CHILD
TRAINING
TIPS

CHILD TRAINING TIPS

WHAT I WISH I KNEW WHEN MY CHILDREN WERE YOUNG

REB BRADLEY

NEW AND UPDATED VERSION

CHILD TRAINING TIPS

Published by WND Books, Washington, D.C. WND Books is a registered trademark of WorldNetDaily, Inc.

Book designed by Mark Karis

WND Books are distributed to the trade by:
Midpoint Trade Books
27 West 20th Street, Suite 1102
New York, New York 10011
WND Books are available at special discounts for bulk purchases. WND Books, Inc.,
also publishes books in electronic formats. For more information call
(541) 474-1776 or visit www.wndbooks.com.

First Edition
Paperback ISBN: 978-1-938067-00-6
eBook ISBN: 978-1-938067-01-3

Library of Congress Catalog-in-Publication Data
Bradley, Reb.
  Child training tips : what I wish I had known when my children were young / Reb Bradley.
-- Millennial Edition.
     pages cm
  ISBN 978-1-938067-00-6 (pbk.)
1. Child rearing--Religious aspects--Christianity. 2. Parenting--Religious aspects--Christianity. 3. Discipline of children. I. Title.
  HQ769.3.B7293 2014
  248.8'45--dc23
                                      2013051146

Printed in the United States of America
14 15 16 17 18 19 EBM 9 8 7 6 5 4 3 2 1

To my wife, Beverly,
and the gifts God has given me:
Nathanael, Anna, Benjamin, Leah,
Michael, and Emily Claire

CONTENTS

ACKNOWLEDGMENTS

I thank the Lord for my wife, Beverly, who was my partner in childrearing. As a fulltime mother, she not only spent more time training our children than I, but she gave many hours reviewing and suggesting edits on the rough draft manuscripts for this book.

I also thank the Lord for my children who endured my limited fatherhood during writing seasons.

I am thankful for Rick Fugate, whom I consider my mentor. It was his book and video series, "What the Bible Says About Child Training," that God used to lay the foundation for biblically based child training I so desperately needed for my family. Without his teaching, I dread to think of where my children would be. This book would never have been written.

I am thankful for the parents of Hope Chapel Sacramento

who, year after year, sat through Rick Fugate's video series with me and gave their input in the many discussions that followed.

I especially thank the Lord for giving us His Word, our only reliable source of Truth.

PREFACE

Many years ago, when the first few of our six children were born, we were hoping they would come with an owner's manual. They didn't, so our first ones were the *experiments*—we did the best we could with what we knew—and we didn't know all that much.

I am definitely not a parent who did everything right—I am actually jealous of people like that. In my journey through rearing our children, I fell into many holes along the way. My aim with this book is to show other parents the locations of the holes and how to get out if they fall in, hence the subtitle, "What I Wish I Knew When My Children Were Young."

This book does *not* have all the answers on child training. It does however, contain answers to many of the questions I had when my oldest children were young. Those looking for an exhaustive manual, balanced in all facets of rearing children, will not find it here. The purpose of this book is simply to expose to parents their possible blind spots, and to offer practical tips and biblically based help in overcoming them. This book has been written primarily for parents of children under twelve years of age, although parents of teens will find valuable help here as well.

Although I have updated this book over the years to present a more complete study on biblical parenting, I recommend the audio or video presentation of my seminar, "Biblical Insights Into Child Training." The seminar covers many of the same topics as this book, but includes stories and illustrations that help humanize the parenting process.

I have published this book in an outline form with many symptom and behavior lists, because I meant it to be a quick-reference manual and supplement for those who have heard the seminar. The reader will notice that a number of points are repeated in different sections. This is because each point is pertinent to its context, and because I didn't want parents to have to reread the entire book to get a complete answer every time they needed help in one area.

A key danger to writing a parenting book consisting primarily of lists of symptoms and cures is that some parents may develop a "cookie-cutter" approach to raising their children. They may lean toward formulaic thinking and relate to each of their children exactly the same. That is the last thing I would desire. I want all parents to be "thinkers" who apply the recommended principles to each of their individual children, taking into account each child's natural disposition and personality. In fact, I am so concerned about the possibility of promoting cookie-cutter thinking that in this edition of the book, I have gone through the entire manuscript and attempted to correct all wording that might promote it.

After receiving overwhelming response to the first editions of this book, I am excited to publish this Millennial Edition. Multitudes of parents have written and told us of how their children radically changed when they began implementing the insights they gained. We are grateful to God for that. Yet, despite the positive response, I have decided to offer a caution to a certain "type" of parent before they begin reading.

So to those of you who might consider yourselves to be *intense* parents—who run your homes like drill sergeants, I offer the following caution: Be forewarned! As you read the pages that follow, you will gain new insights into your children's motives and behaviors, and you may find your usual anger and intolerance growing in intensity the more you read. If that is you, then go slow in implementation! Watch your frustration. Anger is not your friend—it is a detriment to effective parenting. *Love* not *terror* will be your children's greatest motivator.

Keep in mind that our young children are mostly a product of our training, whether by intent or neglect. They are only the way they are because we have not yet finished their training. If the children are not learning fast enough, and the training does not seem to be working, then it is time to look for blind spots in our approach, and not time for greater harshness. Keep in mind God's Word to us through James, " . . . the anger of man does not accomplish the righteousness of God."[1] Children respond best to alert, loving, consistent discipline—not to angry, "don't mess with me, kid," parenting.

May all parents who read this seek God for the insight, self-discipline, and consistency they need to successfully train the next generation to be mature, responsible followers of Christ. Amen.

—*Reb Bradley*

---

1   James 1:20.

INTRODUCTION

"Children today are tyrants. They contradict their parents, they
gobble their food, they terrorize their teachers."
—Socrates, 426 BC

The job of parenting has always been a difficult one, but
those who have lived in America for the last fifty years have
watched it become even more so. Our children are immersed
in a culture that panders to hedonism and are among playmates
that have been raised as narcissists. As parents, we are less confident than our predecessors in our knowledge of raising families.
With the "experts" offering contradictory advice and the lack
of a cohesive, biblical consensus within the Church, Christian
parents have found themselves feeling helpless and frustrated
with their children. For many of them, parenting has become
such a source of frustration that they do everything within their
power to prevent the conception of any more "problems." Their
stress is so great that they count the days until their children are
old enough to go to school or move out on their own. They look

forward to summertime and holiday vacations, but dread the thought of being with their children all day long.

Those parents who are exasperated with their children are missing the blessing that God says children are to bring to their lives. To be blunt, if that is us, we are not perceiving children as a gift, but as a *curse*. Fortunately, it does not have to be that way. When God calls children a "blessing," a "gift," and a "reward,"[1] He places each one in the womb with that potential. If our children are not a blessing to us, it is *not* because an alien tampered with their genetic code as they grew in the womb. It is very possibly because we have not succeeded in some element of their training.

Considering the confusion of contemporary child rearing ideas and the sparse number of solid role models, it is no wonder that we have so many blind spots today. The tragedy is, many frustrated parents believe they are doing everything correctly and think they have no blind spots. *But that is what a blind spot is— something you cannot see!*

One thing is certain, any parents who disavow *any* responsibility for their children's behavior are depriving themselves of the potential they have to shape their children's character and future. May we all be open to see ourselves and our children in the pages that follow.

---

1   Ps. 127:3–5: "Behold, children are a gift of the LORD; the fruit of the womb is a reward. Like arrows in the hand of a warrior, so are the children of one's youth. How blessed is the man whose quiver is full of them; They shall not be ashamed, when they speak with their enemies in the gate."

1

SEVEN OBSTACLES TO SUCCESSFUL PARENTING

I have seen the enemy and he are us.

—Pogo

Before we begin our study in parenting, it will be important for us to identify any obstacles that keep our blind spots hidden. I offer the following seven obstacles, which, if removed, will allow the reader to find greater value in this book.

OBSTACLE 1: PARENTAL DEFENSIVENESS

Regarding our personal lives, many of us recognize our weak human condition and are open to correction from others. However, should someone suggest something is wrong with our children or our parenting, that humility may disappear. We can become highly defensive!

In fact, merely the *suggestion* that we are defensive will cause some of us to immediately defend ourselves. (Some, at this point, are inevitably defending themselves in their minds. If that is *you,*

you may be completely unaware that you are resisting it right now! Blind aren't we?)

In order to gain the most from this book, it will be helpful for you to drop your defenses and admit that you have blind spots and cannot identify them. (If you knew what they were, they wouldn't be "blind" spots; they would be "seen" spots!) One of the main signs of a blind spot is defensiveness. If you read something in this book that contradicts your beliefs or practices, and you *immediately* defend yourself, or attack me, the author, you should consider that your toes have been stepped on and you do not like it. Possibly, you are *unwilling* to even consider that you need to change. You might not actually be wrong, but your intense resistance to "being wrong" could be a sign of defensiveness, which means you are closed to correction, and therefore may miss receiving help with an area of weakness. As the Lord tells us through Solomon, it is the wise who welcome correction and reproof.[1] Let us be wise parents.

Before you continue, would you pause to look at the Lord, and ask Him to open the eyes of your heart.[2]

OBSTACLE 2: CONFUSING RAISING CHILDREN WITH TRAINING THEM

Most parents discover soon after the birth of their first child that parenting is a tremendous responsibility. They feel the weight of caring for a helpless human being, but are often ignorant of their

---

1   Prov. 15:5: "A fool spurns his father's discipline, but whoever heeds correction shows prudence . . . "
Prov. 15:32: "He who ignores discipline despises himself, but whoever heeds correction gains understanding."
Prov. 19:25: "Flog a mocker, and the simple will learn prudence; rebuke a discerning man, and he will gain knowledge."
Prov. 12:1: "Whoever loves discipline loves knowledge, but he who hates correction is stupid." (Also Prov. 9:9; 13:1, 18; 15:12, 31.)

2   Eph. 1:18.

actual job description. As the child grows, they hope they are doing their job correctly, but may find the child is not turning out the way they thought he would. Most parents are like employees who are hired to do a job, but have minimal training, no job descriptions, no plans, and no measurable objectives.

To become an effective *child trainer* requires that a parent understand exactly what God expects them to produce in their children, and how they are to achieve those results. This book should be an aid to formulating a parental job description.

Tragically, most parents have the notion that *raising* children is the same as *training* them. It isn't. "Raising" is providing food and sustenance. It is maintaining life and fostering physical growth. The Scriptures call us not only to raise children, but to *train* them. Those parents who believe they have carried out the biblical injunctions to train their children, yet the children remain unchanged, may have raised and *taught* their children, but they certainly did not succeed in *training* them. By the very definition of "train," that would be impossible.

To train means to *cause a change* in the one being directed. In any place of employment, if a training session is over, but the participants have gained nothing and cannot do the job, they are not regarded as *trained*. They may have been taught, but they were not trained. Any on-the-job training program that lacks results will be examined and reworked. If the military's *basic training* consistently failed to produce skilled soldiers, it would be revamped. If you entrusted your dog to a dog-handler for training, but received it back no different than it was before training, you would be due a refund because the dog had not been successfully trained. *Training* produces results.

The Hebrew word for "rear" (*gadal*) bears out this concept. To *rear* a child literally means "to twist unto greatness." The Hebrew idea of rearing children was to bring them up to maturity by *twisting* them against their nature. Twisting requires firm effort, sustained throughout their childhood, but especially for the first five years.

Consider Proverbs 22:6: "Train up a child in the way he should go: and when he is old, he will not depart from it." God tells parents that long-lasting change requires diligent training. Deuteronomy 6:6–9 reinforces this idea as it admonishes parents to "impress" God's commands on their children.[3] The Hebrew word for *impress* means "to inscribe or etch." According to verses 7–9, this is accomplished by modeling and minute-by-minute instruction in biblical Truths, making a lasting *impression* on them.

Parents who think that proper training of children consists only of playing Christian music to them and teaching them to pray before bedtime and meals will never succeed. Nor will children be trained by simply sending them to Sunday School, youth group, or Christian clubs. Surrounding them with Christian influences is certainly good, but it is no substitute for training. Training is a conscious, active effort of instruction, discipline, and modeling, and not simply a byproduct of a good environment or a loving home. It does not happen by osmosis. Consider that no wild horse was ever trained by being grouped together with trained horses. Neither will our children.[4]

At this point, it is critical to note that although biblically based discipline and instruction can easily shape our children's

---

3   Deut. 6:6–9: "And these words which I command you today shall be in your heart. You shall teach them diligently to your children, and shall talk of them when you sit in your house, when you walk by the way, when you lie down, and when you rise up. You shall bind them as a sign on your hand, and they shall be as frontlets between your eyes. You shall write them on the doorposts of your house and on your gates."

4   Please do not be offended at the comparison of training horses and children. Principles of training are the same, whether the trainee is a soldier, an athlete, a child, or a horse.

behavior, it cannot control their *hearts*. They are not like dogs that can be trained when young and will remain trained for the rest of their lives with occasional reinforcement. No, children are not animals—they are self-determining individuals who will one day grow up and decide what they will do with the childhood training they received.

Parents who want to have continued influence into their child's teen years will need to know how to transition from *authoritarian*-based influence to leadership rooted in *love* and *respect*. More on that in chapter 17.

OBSTACLE 3: MISUNDERSTANDING HUMAN DEPRAVITY

One dangerous, humanistic idea that has crept into the Church is that children are basically good and need only be loved and cared for to bring out that good. This view not only ignores the basic teaching of Scripture, but encourages parents to let a child's nature take its own course. That is tantamount to taking a wild skunk as a pet, believing it will never release its stench because of the good home you will give it. The Bible teaches that allowing a self-centered heart to take its natural course brings heartache to parents.[5]

God has spoken clearly in the Scriptures about the depraved nature of humanity. Jeremiah 17:9 tells us that "the heart is deceitful above all things and beyond cure." In Genesis 6:5, we read that "The LORD saw how great man's wickedness on the earth had become, and that every inclination of the thoughts of his heart was *only evil all the time*" (Emphasis is mine). The sinful inclinations of mankind do not kick in after puberty, but

---

5   Prov. 29:15: "The rod and rebuke give wisdom, but a child left to himself brings shame to his mother."

according to Genesis 8:21, " . . . every inclination of his heart is evil from childhood."[6]

King David, a man after God's own heart, understood that he was "sinful at birth, sinful from the time my mother conceived me,"[7] and he declared that from birth we go astray, even coming out of the womb "speaking lies."[8]

For parents to successfully train children, they must understand Proverbs 22:15: "Foolishness is bound up in the heart of a child . . . " The Hebrew word for foolishness is *'ivveleth*, which does not mean childish immaturity or silliness, but rather *perversity*, which spawns *deviousness, defiance,* and *rebellion.* In describing teens and adults who grew up without proper training, Solomon called them fools[9] using the word *keciyl*, which, in its root, means "fat"; in other words, bloated with or full up of *self.*

The parents who think their child is just a little angel and would rarely do anything really wrong will not adequately apply themselves to the task of child training and are guaranteed by the Scriptures to reap grief in the years to come. Consider Solomon's words: "A foolish son brings grief to his father and bitterness to the one who bore him."[10] "To have a fool for a son brings grief; there is no joy for the father of a fool."[11] And " . . . a child left to himself disgraces his mother."[12]

---

6   Consider also Eccles. 7:20, 29; Ps. 14:2–3; Job 4:17–19; 15:15–16; 25:4–6; Isa. 59:7; 64:6; Jer. 13:23; Mark 7:20–23; John 2:24–25; Rom. 3:10–18; 7:18.

7   Ps. 51:5.

8   Ps. 58:3.

9   Prov. 10:1; 15:20; 17:21, 25; 19:13.

10   Prov. 17:25.

11   Prov. 17:21.

12   Prov. 29:15.

What parents must absolutely understand is that each child is born with a narcissistic, hedonistic nature. That is, each one of us comes into the world consumed with *ourselves* (narcissism) and preoccupied with *gratification* and *pleasure* (hedonism). By nature, we all want to say "yes" to everything we want, but it is the job of parents to train us to say "no" to ourselves through discipline and instruction. Parents' primary responsibility is to train their children against their self-oriented nature.

Unfortunately, since the mid-1940s, child development "experts" have lost sight of this all-important truth. Modern parenting philosophies fail to equip parents with what children need most in the early years. This is why America has seen a steady loss of moral fiber in the last five decades. Not only are families falling apart; not only have sexually immoral relationships become "normal"; not only have STD infections become epidemic; but crime has skyrocketed as well. According to FBI statistics, since 1960, violent crime is up more than 300 percent, theft and murder are up more than 250 percent, and illegal drug use is up more than 400 percent. Not only are parents raising more juvenile delinquents, cheaters, and criminals since they began embracing modern parenting philosophies, but we have seen an extreme loss of moral fiber in every area of life. The narcissism, hedonism, and entitlement thinking of modern teens is a direct result of parents who did not know how to train their children against their natural bents.

Although God's Word is a sufficient source for understanding a child's depraved nature, it is interesting to note the conclusions of the Minnesota Crime Commission, which issued the following report after years of studying the relationship of environment to crime:

> Every baby starts life as a little savage. He is completely selfish and self-centered. He wants what he wants when he wants it: his bottle, his mother's attention, his playmate's toys, his uncle's

watch, or whatever. Deny him these and he seethes with rage and aggressiveness which would be murderous were he not so helpless. He's dirty, he has no morals, no knowledge, no developed skills. This means that all children, not just certain children, but all children are born delinquent. If permitted to continue in their self-centered world of infancy, given free reign to their impulsive actions to satisfy every want, every child would grow up a criminal, a thief, a killer, a rapist.[13]

The parents who desire to see their children grow in godly character must not assume it will happen because they are being raised in a loving Christian home. Successful training of a self-centered child requires hard work, great personal sacrifice, and prayer. Love must be present, but by itself it is not enough.

OBSTACLE 4: TRUST IN WORLDLY "EXPERTS"

As children of God, we have been given the Scriptures as our only reliable source of absolute truth.[14] The world offers many ideas it regards to be "true," but the Bible is the one standard for determining what is *actually* True. The Word encapsulates our knowledge of God, and is the means by which He has given us "everything we need for life and godliness."[15] For basic parenting principles, therefore, we must look primarily to God's Word. To look elsewhere guarantees trouble.

Psalm 1:1 tells us that we will be blessed if we do not seek advice from those without Christ. Although they have the appearance of wisdom and offer insights that may seem reasonable, their

---

13 Minnesota Crime Commission Report; *Journal of the American Institute of Criminal Law and Criminology,* Vol. 18, No. 1 (May 1927).

14 2 Tim. 3:16.

15 2 Pet. 1:3.

thinking is infected with worldliness, and leads to regret.[16] The apostle Paul emphasized this when he pointed out that those without Christ lack genuine wisdom, and what they offer as valuable, God regards as worthless.[17] He says that " . . . the wisdom of this world is foolishness in God's sight . . . the thoughts of the wise are vain."[18] That should not surprise us, considering that God tells us that those lacking the fear of God, whether professing Christian or not, are hampered in their thinking and do not have even the basics of wisdom.[19] These warnings are validated by America's present condition. The breakdown of the family and the resulting corruption of our society is partially a result of the last few generations receiving guidance from worldly "experts." Like the rest of American society, families within the Church are also in decline, because Christian leaders have undiscerningly received "wisdom" from the world's experts, then Christianized it and passed it on to the Church.

With God's Word offering such an abundant resource of absolute Truth and godly wisdom, we must draw our basic principles for child training strictly from the Bible. Although most Christians will quickly agree with this premise, many are unaware of the worldly ideas they have incorporated into their parenting. It would, therefore, benefit every parent to reevaluate and determine the validity of their present child training philosophies in light of biblical principles.

As an example, worldly experts observe rebellion in two-year-olds and deduce that all children naturally go through a phase that they label the "terrible twos." They then encourage parents to not

---

16   Prov. 16:25: "There is a way that seems right to a man, but its end is the way of death."

17   1 Cor. 1:19–25.

18   1 Cor. 3:19–20.

19   Prov. 9:10; 1:7; Ps. 111:10.

be concerned, but to patiently wait for the phase to run its course. When that child is still defiant at age three, the concerned parents are told not to worry, because the child is simply going through a phase called the "trying threes." When the child is still willful and demanding at adolescence, the parents are told that it is a transitory prepubescent phase, but will eventually pass. By the time the child becomes a teenager, his parents already believe the modern idea that teens are naturally rebellious and independent from their families. They endure disrespectful attitudes, hoping that their teen will grow out of his self-absorption before their hearts break.

Sadly, many parents accept from the "experts" that these phases are natural and unavoidable. They expect them and endure them, not realizing that God's Word not only does not recognize any such "phases" of rebellion that should be tolerated, but teaches parents how to prevent rebellion. Those who choose not to accept modern phases in their children, and instead implement biblical principles, discover that their children never go through them. One must conclude that the experts who developed ideas about childhood "phases" studied only poorly trained children. At the least, they did not take into consideration that these phases are common to this century and primarily to affluent nations like America.

Upon hearing biblical principles taught, some parents wrestle with accepting them. If that is you, then as you read, listen to your reason for your struggle. Is it that you believe the Bible teaches something different? Is it that you dispute the meaning of the Hebrew words cited? Or could it be that you have based your convictions on human ideas and worldly principles, or possibly on your own experience? As God's people, we must grow in our knowledge and application of God's Word, and base our convictions on its precepts. Parenting practices rooted in any other premise will always fail. As you read on, may you take to heart that which comes from God's Word—the rest, consider seriously.

OBSTACLE 5: FEAR OF REPEATING ONE'S OWN PAST NEGATIVE CHILDHOOD

Some parents approach child training with a "vendetta." They are out to right the wrongs they experienced as children themselves. The frustration they feel from their childhood memories, however, often creates a blind spot. Consequently, biblical elements of child training may be inadvertently avoided, because they seem too much like what they endured.

A parent's vendetta may be rooted in a variety of childhood hurts:

- The adult who grew up in a poor family is determined to indulge his children with all that he did not have, yet cannot now understand why his children are turning out self-centered, ungrateful, and entitled.

- The adult who was never allowed to play or do social activities as a child may require little work of his own children, and may overindulge them with sports and recreation. He then wonders why they are lazy or preoccupied with themselves and their personal gratification.

- The adult whose parents were too strict or abusive is tempted to be too permissive with his own children, despite the clear teaching of Scripture.

- The adult who was never allowed to speak his mind to his parents takes the opposite approach in his home, and then finds he is raising sassy, smart-mouthed children.

- The adult who was never given wisdom behind parental commands is determined with his own children to offer full explanations before they are expected to obey. Yet, finds that as his children grow, they are unable to obey without arguing, his explanations seeming to serve as invitations to debate.

The poor training of any child is a tragic thing, but it is made worse when that child grows up and hurts his own children by trying too hard to do the opposite of what was done to him. Those parents who were victims of poor training are right to avoid the mistakes made by their parents, but they must guard themselves from rejecting solid biblical principles just because they seem *close* to what they experienced. If our parents' approach *seemed* close to biblical parenting, yet bore bad fruit, we can be certain it was not biblical. God preserved in His Word exactly the right principles we need for training children, and parents who accurately implement them will not be disappointed. In fact, they will be blessed.

OBSTACLE 6: SURVIVAL-ORIENTED PARENTING

Some parents are reading this book because their children are young and they simply want to learn how to train them. Many parents, however, have older children and want help in *surviving* them. Self-preservation is the driving force for many a mom and dad.

You know this is *you* if the highlight of your day is when the kids finally fall asleep. Your big thrill comes when you slump into a chair and think to yourself, "I'm still alive." But your elation disappears when you remember, "I have to get up in the morning and do it all over again!"

Survival-oriented parenting is the most exhausting and counterproductive approach to child rearing possible, because it focuses on *us* and not the *children*. It is entirely *defensive*. For training to be successful, it must be proactive and purposed in training them for their good—not our sanity.

For this book to be of the most value, parents must allow the Lord to reprogram their minds to think *proactively*. They must have a new purpose—not to *survive* the children, but to *train* them biblically. Consider the hope-giving words of Solomon:

"Discipline your son, and he will give you peace; he will bring delight to your soul" (Proverbs 29:17).

Biblically trained children do not have to be simply endured or survived, they impart to their parents *peace* and bring *delight* to their souls. Did you follow that? If *properly* trained, children will actually impart to us peace and bring us delight. Instead of continually draining our emotional reserves, they encourage and lift us up.

Survival-oriented parents have good things to look forward to if they are willing to turn from self-protective parenting and concentrate on biblical training and discipline of their children.

OBSTACLE 7: A FORMULAIC APPROACH TO PARENTING

We live in an age when impatience and love of expedience characterize our outlook on life. Consequently, we search for self-help books that promise easy methods to solve every problem, whether it is codependence, marital strife, or financial stress. Magazines offer ten steps to truer love, tighter abs, or greater happiness. We have been conditioned to look to steps, principles, and methods for quick success in all areas of life. Even in the church, we want the tricks to accelerated growth, better leadership, and more fruitful evangelism.

This means that many are reading this book in search of the ultimate parenting formula. Unfortunately, they won't find it here. Or should I say, "fortunately" it isn't here.

A formulaic approach to parenting is one of the greatest hindrances to fruitful child training. Formulas, after all, involve mixing ingredients and following precise steps to produce a specific result, time after time. This is great in science, horticulture, and cooking, but cannot be applied to matters of the human heart. Our children are self-determining individuals whose hearts can be *influenced*, but not *controlled*.

As I will discuss later in this book, behavior can be controlled to a great degree, but we must not confuse *controlling* behavior with *influencing* hearts. If we think we have the power to control exactly how our children turn out, we will rely too much upon ourselves and our ability to intimidate. We will subject our children to our chosen parenting process, relegating them to mere ingredients in a formula. When that happens, they cease to be *people* and become *things*. And when that happens, the relationship that is needed to influence their hearts breaks down. Many obedient Christian children have grown up and gone prodigal because their parents concentrated more on controlling them with authority than influencing them through love and acceptance.

Parents, as you begin this book, keep in mind that your children are not soulless animals to be trained. Neither are they chemicals in a formula that can be processed for guaranteed results. It is critical that we realize our children are people whose hearts, as they reach adolescence, are influenced more by relationship than by external controls. In all our intensity, we must treat them as fellow humans, and not as dehumanized ingredients in a cake we are baking.[20]

As you read this book about training behavior, keep in mind that it will be our love for our children that gains us the most influence over who they become.

---

20   Adapted from *Solving the Crisis in Homeschooling*, p. 82, 2013.

2

GOALS OF CHILD TRAINING

To understand . . . principles of human behavior . . . we must first begin by accepting the basic premise that all humans are born hedonists (aka narcissists) and have an intrinsic need to seek pleasure, avoid pain, and engage in those activities that best accomplish both with the least amount of effort.

—*Dr. Terry G. Shaw*[1]

We are all born emotional, passionate beings. We come into the world determined to survive and we vehemently express ourselves to get what we need: "Waaa!" and Momma feeds us; "Waaa!" and our diaper is changed; "Waaa!" and we are put down for a nap. As infants, our strong will can keep us comfortable and alive—the more outspoken we are, the more our needs are met. However, as we start to grow, we no longer cry only for necessities—we crave pleasure, too. At nine months old, if it's Uncle Bert's watch we want, we grab on and scream when he does not give it to us. Uncle Bert might laugh and marvel at our strength, but he easily pulls his watch away, sparking our anger. We are so furious that if we were seven feet

---

1   Terry G. Shaw, PhD, ABPN, "When Teens Struggle in School," http://www.nbdaok.com/articles/1.htm.

tall and coordinated, Uncle Bert would be dead, and we would have his watch. The will *to* survive that kept us alive as newborns is revealed as a will to be gratified, the older we grow.

We must understand the self-centered drive of human nature. From birth, we are all driven by *passion*—we want what we want, when we want it, and we refuse things we do not want. Hence, as young children, we beg or scream for ice cream, and turn our noses up at Brussels sprouts. By nature, we hate having to wait and demand immediate gratification—we throw fits when we do not get our way. From our first year of life, we want to gratify ourselves and loathe the idea of reaping consequences for our actions. If left unsubdued, every child's will to be gratified will escalate in strength.[2]

Our culture is in a moral mess today because parents have not understood that their primary job is to give children victory over their narcissistic and hedonistic tendencies. Moms and dads have no clear goal in their parenting, so accidentally strengthen their children's natural self-centeredness.

It is my observation that most Christian parents have no clearly defined moral, emotional, or spiritual goals in their parenting. They tell their children about the Lord and His ways, but they lack a clearly defined goal for that training. They know they want their children to know God and to have godly character, but they are not sure what the final product is supposed to look like. It is as though they are baking a dessert, yet don't know if it is an ice cream cake or a peach cobbler, and they keep throwing in sweet ingredients, hoping the results will be edible. It would be far better for parents to define their goal and then create a plan to accomplish it. There is truth to the saying, "If you aim

---

2   Adapted in part from page 20 of *Born Liberal Raised Right,* WND Books, 2008.

at nothing, you will always hit it." Parents must have a clearly defined target for their children's growth.

In order to determine if we are accomplishing God's goals for child rearing, we must first identify them. As Christian parents, our most obvious goal is to bring our children into an intimate relationship with Christ, so that as they grow, they will be motivated by their own love for God. Second to that, God's most basic goal for training children is encapsulated in Ephesians 6:4. There, parents are told regarding their children, "...bring them up in the training and instruction of the Lord." The Greek word for "bring them up" holds the key. That word is *ektrepho*, which means *to rear up to maturity*. The primary goal then, of training and instruction, is to rear up children to be *mature*. For us to bring children to maturity will require that we have a clear definition of what maturity is.

WHAT IS MATURITY?

Based on a broad study of the Scriptures and a concentrated study of Proverbs, I have concluded that maturity is characterized by three elements: *self-control*,[3] *wisdom*,[4] and *responsibility*,[5] which can be defined as follows:[6]

A *self-controlled* person has all normal human passions, but is not ruled by them. A self-controlled child is one who is able to obey Mommy the first time when called. It is a self-controlled child who is able to not touch something that belongs to others

---

3   Prov. 29:11; 14:16; 21:20; 22:15; 26:11; 12:16, 23; 13:16; 29:20.

4   Prov. 10:21; 29:15; 17:16; 18:2; 12:15.

5   Prov. 17:16; 6:6; 24:30; 26:6; 26:16.

6   Adapted from chapter 3 of *Born Liberal, Raised Right*, WND Books, 2008.

or not sneak candy when Daddy's back is turned. Such a child may be angered when teased, but will have the self-restraint to not respond with violence. The bottom line is that a child with self-control has the ability to say "no" to himself and "yes" to what is right. The child who is allowed to grow up without self-restraint may reach adulthood, but will remain a big "kid"—absorbed with himself, pleasure, fun, and entertainment, sometimes at the expense of those around him. Whatever he thinks or feels is of supreme importance, and he, therefore, will be prone to saying whatever is on his mind, whether respectful or not, and will pursue whatever appeals to his passions. His self-centeredness will make him arrogant, impatient, demanding, and ungrateful. He will be unable to easily delay gratification. One without self-restraint will lack a selfless concern for others, which is critical for healthy families and communities.

A *wise* person is not the same as a *smart* person whose intelligence is innate. Many highly educated, brilliant people make foolish choices every day—their rational thinking skills impaired by their passions and drives. A person who is truly wise is one who learns from mistakes, makes sound decisions, and handles stressful problems with a level head. More importantly, people with wisdom are *rational*, because passions are not clouding their thinking. For example, when our craving for illicit sexual experiences causes us to pursue gratification without regard to the consequences, we have not acted in wisdom, but in fact, have become quite the fool. When our craving for alcohol is so great that we sneak to hide our booze and lie to cover our actions, even when sober we make foolish choices that affect everyone around us. When our compulsion to play the lottery or to buy that new dress causes us to spend money that should have been spent on rent, we and others suffer from our unwise choices. Unless a child is raised to say "no" to his passions or whims, he will never walk in the wisdom necessary for maturity. In fact, because that which rules us colors our outlook on life, the child and others raised like him will see life through the cloudy eyes of passion. He will view himself as insightful and wise, when in actuality, he is the opposite, because his perspective is skewed by his passions. A *responsible* person is one who accepts personal accountability for his own actions. He does not make excuses or blame others for his failures, and does not expect others to pay the consequences for his mistakes. He takes responsibility for himself and pays his own bills in life. A responsible person is faithful and conscientious in work habits. Such integrity and reliability, however, are only possible when passions are not in charge. When a child's desire for fun is greater than his sense of duty, he will compulsively play when it is time to work, and when he grows up, he will produce poorly for his employer. When a child is not held responsible to fulfill his personal duties, but is given "another chance" time and again, he grows up thinking that everyone else is responsible to bail him out. He thinks he should not have to live with the consequences of his actions, and comes to develop a "victim" mentality—nothing is ever his fault—someone else is always to blame for his misery. He sees himself as not responsible for the results of his choices or of his reactions to life. In fact, he insists he has a right to that which he has not earned, and is entitled to be given that for which others have worked.

So the primary goal of parenting is to raise children to be *mature*, having the traits of *self-control, wisdom,* and *responsibility.* The young person whose life reflects these traits will be ready for adulthood, and the society whose citizens reflect such character will benefit as well. Many parents of the last fifty years have not made instilling these traits their primary goal, so their children have reached adulthood, but have not matured past childhood. They may be responsible enough to function with independence, but their conduct in relationships, at work, and in society reflects a lack of emotional and moral maturity.

The problem in modern America is that most parents assume maturity to be a byproduct of getting older. Consequently, few make significant efforts to develop it within their children. In fact, most would have difficulty even defining maturity, and therefore, are unable to effectively cultivate it. Parents who do want to help their kids become mature often confuse maturity with "independence" and grant their immature children autonomy early in life. They do not realize that an immature person granted independence does not develop the self-restraint of maturity, but regresses deeper into the self-indulgence of *immaturity*. They may develop survival skills and talk like they are peers of adults, but they will not grow in maturity. Parents must, therefore, understand maturity and make a conscious effort to train their children in its attributes.

HOW IS MATURITY DEVELOPED?

The key to becoming mature is found in the book of Hebrews. There we read about the path Christ had to walk in order to become mature. The primary Greek word for mature is *teleioo*, which is often translated as *perfect*, but in fact means *complete*, *whole*, or *mature*.[7] For Christ to reach maturity, he had to walk a path of *suffering*.

> In bringing many sons to glory, it was fitting that God, for whom and through whom everything exists, should make the author of their salvation *perfect [mature] through suffering*. (Hebrews 2:10, emphasis mine)

---

7   It does not mean flawless or without corruption.

Although he was a son, he *learned obedience from what he suffered and, once made perfect* [mature], he became the source of eternal salvation for all who obey him. (Hebrews 5:8, emphasis mine)

Maturity is developed only by facing challenges and learning to overcome them. It is like a destination that can only be reached by traveling the hard road that leads there. Travelers will definitely not arrive if a path of ease is taken. In fact, all other routes lead away from maturity.

This principle of growing through challenges is true in much of life. Hence the saying, "An athlete unchallenged is an athlete unchanged." Athletes only grow stronger and more capable when they face increasingly greater opponents or subject themselves to more and more rigorous exercises. This is why the apostle Paul compared Christian maturity to a prize won by a disciplined athlete.[8]

In the same way, our children will only develop maturity if they are faced with challenges. If we protect them from all suffering, they may grow up, but they will never mature. We must therefore be certain that they learn to handle the suffering of broccoli and the misery of cleaning their rooms. They must learn from us that they can find contentment, even when they don't get their way.

When parents orchestrate challenges for their child, it cultivates in him self-discipline and self-control as he learns to submit himself to their leadership. As we have discussed, matu-

---

8   1 Cor. 9:25–26: "Everyone who competes in the games goes into strict training. They do it to get a crown that will not last; but we do it to get a crown that will last forever. Therefore I do not run like a man running aimlessly; I do not fight like a man beating the air."

rity is rooted primarily in self-control, which, in turn, facilitates growth in *wisdom* and *responsibility*. The most basic objective of training children, therefore, is the subduing of our children's self-will. From the time children are born, parents must develop in them the ability to say "no" to their own desires and "yes" to their parents. That is why parental control of young children is imperative. A child who learns to deny his own desires and submit to his parent's controls, gains inner controls. Children are born into the world self-centered (narcissistic), and so must be trained from infancy that the world does not revolve around them. They must learn from their parents that life will not always give them their way. Susanna Wesley, an eighteenth-century mother of nine, famous for her wisdom, put it this way:

> The parent who studies to subdue [self-will] in his child works together with God in the renewing and saving a soul. The parent who indulges it does the devil's work, makes religion impossible, salvation unattainable, and does all that in him lies to damn his child, soul and body forever.[9]

The child whose will is never subdued when young, comes to believe that he should have *what* he wants, *when* he wants it, and should not have to endure *anything* he does not like. He will grow older thinking he is being deprived whenever he does not get what he wants from life, and by his teen years, he will develop an entitlement mentality and know little of personal responsibility. The indulged child is frequently angry because he does not get what he thinks is owed him. Ultimately, he will develop a "victim" mentality—nothing is ever his fault—someone else is always to blame for his misery.

---

9   *The Journal of John Wesley* (Chicago: Moody, n. d.), p. 106.

Since most parents, even Christian parents, believe maturity is an inevitable part of growing up, they content themselves to love their kids, take them to church, and try to give them a happy childhood. They do little to help the process, and without realizing it—much to hurt it. All children, unless calamity occurs, *will* grow older, but only those groomed toward maturity will attain it. Hence, as parents, we must work diligently to help our children develop the qualities leading to maturity.

WHAT CHARACTERIZES IMMATURITY?

To further clarify the definition of maturity, we must understand *immaturity*. The child whose will is not subdued in the first few years of life will be greatly hampered in the maturing process. No matter how old he gets, a strong self-will ruled by the craving for *self-indulgence* (hedonism) will be the mark of his immaturity. Sadly, hedonism characterizes most children today—even in Christian families. As caring parents, it is especially important for us to identify and eliminate that in our child rearing which feeds the will to be gratified and fosters hedonism.

WHAT ARE SIGNS OF IMMATURITY AND SELF-INDULGENCE?

Immaturity is chiefly characterized by *narcissism* and *hedonism.* *Narcissism*, simply defined, is an excessive sense of self-importance, characterized by self-preoccupation, self-centeredness, and inflated self-love. It is a self-oriented worldview that makes selfless love for others impossible. *Hedonism* is devotion to the pursuit of pleasure, gratification, and personal fulfillment. Hedonists have an extreme aversion to deprivation of pleasure, which they regard as *suffering.* The main difference between narcissists and hedonists is that a hedonist *lives* for pleasure while a narcissist believes pleasure is his *right.* Consider the following traits of immaturity. Do these symptoms characterize your children?

They Lack Self-restraint

- Self-indulgent people rarely say "no" to themselves.

- They have a difficult time doing anything in moderation which gratifies, and frequently overdo it.

- They are driven by passion, whether it is anger, lust, gluttony, pride, covetousness, etc. They cannot delay gratification.

- They do whatever they feel like, or are so used to having their way that they think they *should* have whatever they want.

- The satisfaction of their *own* will is foremost in their life—others are considered second, if at all.

They Are Self-absorbed

- Self-centeredness so rules self-indulgent people that they live as if the world revolves around them—life is interpreted by how it affects *them*.

- Whenever self-centered children approach their parents with a question, (which may be frequent), it usually involves something they want for themselves. The well-being of others is rarely on their minds.

- May think of others, but only after satisfying themselves.

- Those who are self-consumed push and lobby parents constantly to get what they want, and persist even after being refused.

- Insist on their "rights" to personal decisions and living their "own life."

- Think they deserve everything that is given to them, and are unappreciative despite the feelings of others; not easily satisfied.

- They are seldom happy; complain and whine a majority of the time; often discontent.

- Discontent with food or other gifts set before them.

- They are quite hedonistic, preoccupied with fun and self-gratification.

- Expect for life to be exciting; demand entertainment; frequently bored.

- Expect to have their own way; express blatant irritation when desires are thwarted.

- Impatient; demand others' immediate attention; low tolerance for waiting.

They Lack Wisdom

- Their desire for gratification rules them, affecting all of their decisions, actions, and reactions; they are impulsive and lack discretion.

- They may be very smart but make foolish choices, because their reasoning faculties are clouded by their passions and obsessions.

- They consistently squander money (or save it with the intent of spending it on themselves.)

- They do not learn from their mistakes; they repeatedly get into trouble for the same offense.

- In response to attacks and offenses from younger siblings, they retaliate as if they were small children themselves.

- When confronted by problems, they foolishly "bury their heads in the sand" and pretend the problem will go away.

- They cannot be left alone and trusted to make wise choices; their compulsion to pursue gratification robs their thoughts of clarity.

They Are Irresponsible

- When they make mistakes, they habitually deny their responsibility.

- Nothing is ever their fault. In their minds, they are always victims of others' failures. Someone or something else is to blame.

- When they get caught for breaking the rules, they do not see their penalty as a consequence of their choices, but hold responsible the one who caught them or turned them in.

- Even their anger is someone else's fault.

- They resent work or anything that requires self-discipline.

- They compulsively play, even as adults.

- They are lazy; they habitually play during chore time, and look for ways to get out of work.

- They despise opportunities to serve others, particularly their siblings.

- The thought of serving others rarely crosses their mind.

- In response to assigned chores, they roll their eyes; complain; disappear before, during, and after task; do as little as possible.

- After completion of assigned tasks, refuse to ask, "Is there anything more I can do?"

Some parents read a list like this and respond with excitement—their children are on the right path! Others, however, will respond with discouragement—they *thought* their children were heading in a good direction, but now realize they are off course. Parents, do not despair! Thank the Lord for a timely course correction. Yes, there is work to be done, but effort invested into developing maturity is never wasted.

USING THE GOAL OF MATURITY AS A BASIS FOR PARENTAL DECISIONS

To restate our premise—a proper understanding of maturity and immaturity is foundational to effective parenting, for without a clear understanding of the goals of parenting, we have no frame of reference for parental decisions. To evaluate our parenting decisions, we need simply determine: Which will this activity, organization, entertainment, relationship, etc., foster within our children—maturity or immaturity? It is really that simple.

The problem is that we mistakenly make it our primary goal to give our children happy and fulfilling childhoods. Consequently, we feed their narcissism and accidentally keep them immature. By the time they reach their teen years, they are just like the other "normal" self-involved teenagers whose parents also made a fun childhood *their* chief goal. Since so many parents indulge their children, America is filled with immature, gratification-oriented teenagers. Researchers and experts, not realizing that teenage rebellion and self-absorption is a phenomena of the last one hundred years, and unique to only affluent nations like ours, have concluded such behavior is a natural and temporary phase of growing up. Parents expect it and accept it. Most teens do grow up, but sadly, too few become mature.

Although most of us as parents love our children, our efforts to make them happy and win their affection harm them. Indulged children are unprepared for the challenges of adulthood because their parents sent the message that their personal happiness is of supreme importance. As adults, they will think they are entitled to be rescued from life's challenges. They will lack the self-discipline necessary for successful employment, and their self-centeredness will cause strife in their marriages. Then when their marriages fail, they will consider themselves innocent "victims" of their *spouse's* shortcomings.

From the time they are young, we must prepare our children

for the hardships they will face in life. They will find that true fulfillment does not come from a glut of fun and entertainment and getting your way, but from responsibility and serving others. They will find security and derive happiness from a home marked by firm boundaries and love. I promise.

WHAT HAS LIFE TAUGHT US?

Those of us who have lived at least twenty-five years have learned that life is hard, things don't always go our way, and we don't always get what we want in life. Our children must be prepared in their youth for the challenges they will find in the real world. They must learn that they cannot have everything they want, and that they can endure quite well with less than they hoped for. To mature properly, children must be trained while they are still toddlers to obey their parents without resistance, and they must learn that they can survive suffering through the trials of life, such as Brussels sprouts and picking up their toys. With their parents' help, they can learn as early as possible to die to themselves,[10] preparing them to live for Christ. Otherwise, as teenagers, they will remain self-consumed, rebellious, and far from God. May we as parents be faithful to do what is right.

---

10   Col. 3:5; Rom. 12:1; 8:13; 6:6–8, 13; 1 Cor. 9:26–27; Gal. 5:24; Titus 2:12; Eph. 4:22; Matt. 16:24–26; Luke 14:26.

3

ESTABLISHING CONTROL IN THE HOME

When the Duke of Windsor was asked what impressed him most in America, he replied, *"The way American parents obey their children."*[1]

Today, some parents are afraid to keep their children under control, because "controlling" others is purported to be a psychological "no no"—*controlling*, they have heard, is "abusing." Parents are afraid that if they require their child to do what he is told, he will grow up with a warped psyche. Then he'll go into therapy, write a book against them, and discuss it as a guest on TV talk shows.

Christian parents need not fear they will harm their children if they train them to obey. The fifth commandment requires children to honor and obey their mother and father.[2] "Children, obey your parents in the Lord, for this is right. 'Honor your father and mother'—which is the first commandment with a

---

1   *Look* magazine, March 5, 1957. Emphasis mine.

2   Exod. 20:12; Deut. 5:16; Eph. 6:1–3.

promise—'that it may go well with you and that you may enjoy long life on the earth'" (Ephesians 6:1–3).

God promises *blessings* to obedient children, not *harm*. Like all the other commandments, the responsibility to enforce it falls to parents, so it is their job to exercise firm control over their children and train them to be obedient.

Please understand, there is no need to fear that requiring children to obey you will harm them. You don't need *permission* to offer your children strong leadership—you have the *admonishment* of God. Bringing our children under our control is biblical, bears good fruit, and is therefore wise.

WHAT IS A CONTROLLED CHILD?

A child under parental control is one who has submitted his will to his parents. He has accepted his parents' role as leaders and his as follower. When they speak to him, he obeys quickly and with a good attitude—even when they are not watching. He has self-control, so obeys them without sass or complaint.

Think of an obedient child like you would a good employee. A good worker is one who respects his employer and abides by his rules. He raises his hand to humbly offer ideas at a company meeting and doesn't talk back to his boss even when he thinks him wrong or unwise. He shows up to work on time and works diligently whether he is being watched or not. A good employee has accepted his employer's authority to lead.

The best biblical example of this kind of submission is the Son of God who modeled respect and subjection of will with His Father in Heaven. If you recall, in the days before His crucifixion, Jesus did not look forward to the suffering He would face on the cross, so He pled with His Heavenly Father to change His mind: "Father, if you are willing, take this cup from me; yet not my will, but yours be done."[3] Jesus tried to change His Father's mind and demonstrated proper submission when He made clear that He would accept what His Father decided. He showed us that a well-behaved, well-balanced child is not that way because He has been squashed by His parents, but because it was His choice to submit His will to them.

During His ministry, when Jesus's heavenly Father directed Him, He didn't postpone obedience or comply half-heartedly, but did whatever He was told: "I do exactly what my Father has commanded me . . ."[4] A child under parental control obeys quickly, doing precisely what he is instructed to do. And as Jesus modeled, he does it exactly how it should be done: ". . . I do nothing on my own but speak just what the Father has taught me."[5]

The attitude and spirit of a child under parental control says, "Whatever you say Mommy. What's important is not what *I* want Dad, but what *you* want for me. *You're* in charge—not *me*." A child under parental control has learned by instruction and discipline that his parents are the leaders and he is the follower.

Such a child can be called to dinner just one time and he immediately comes, and may even ask, "What can I do to help?" A child under parental control can be calmly instructed to go to bed and he says, "Yes, Mom," or "Sure, Dad," and heads to bed with no fuss. He accepts his role as the follower—not the co-leader who has a right to offer his ideas.

Some parents read this and imagine such sweet behavior is a lofty dream. If that is you, then please understand it is not only possible, but must be a reality or you will raise your children to

---

3   Luke 22:42.

4   John 14:31b.

5   John 8:28b and John 12:50b.

be typical narcissistic, entitled teenagers. Children don't have to grow up to be self-absorbed, mouthy monsters.

ESTABLISHING PARENTAL CONTROL

Establishing parental control in the home means training your children to recognize and respect your authority in their lives. It is clarifying to them that they are not part of the parental leadership team and you do not need them to help you run the home. A child under parental control grasps that you are the *leaders* and they are the *followers*. It is critical that parents train their children to consistently submit to parental authority without question for a number of reasons.

Why Control Is Important in Training

1. Quick obedience to parental authority must be learned early on to ensure safety in times of danger. We cannot wait until our toddlers run into traffic, touch a hot stove, or chase after a strange dog to teach them to respond to our instructions. If we want our children kept safe, we must train them to obey quickly every time we speak. Otherwise, they will obey only when we scream.

2. The optimum success of any training requires that the will of the trainee be submitted to the trainer. To permit resistance in a trainee will frustrate everyone and hinder learning. A willful child who reaches his teen years still defiant never accepted his parents' authority to make decisions in his life.

3. Control of a child is necessary, because it is what develops self-discipline—the key trait of maturity. As a child is required to function within firm boundaries, and infractions are consistently reinforced by disciplinary consequences, he develops the ability to say "no" to himself and "yes" to what's right. The *outer* controls imposed give him *inner* controls. Keep in mind the original *Karate Kid*: "Wax on, wax off . . . wax on, wax off . . ."

4. Children need firm boundaries, and cannot be allowed to push and whine, constantly voicing their opinions about discipline, personal duties, or family decisions, because they are actually being permitted to assume responsibility for running the home—a task for which God has not equipped their small shoulders.

5. The stress from helping their parents run the home and testing the limits causes children to have a generally unhappy disposition, which means that they will be more argumentative and inclined to conflicts with their siblings. Consistently required obedience removes stress and gives children a sense of security and peace.

6. A child who is accustomed to pushing and getting his own way at home has greater difficulty in submitting to any authority outside the home, including teachers, employers, and police. Great numbers of people have been tased and arrested just because they never learned to close their mouths and do what they were told while growing up. Parents sometimes mean well but harm their children by permitting them to resist parental leadership.

7. The greatest reason to train children in the area of self-control is that a child who has learned submission to human authority more easily submits to God's authority when he grows up. Adults who profess faith in Christ, yet do not obey Him without question and yield to His authority, very likely grew up without learning to submit quickly to authority. They inadvertently were trained to resist authority by not being required to obey it.

It is important to understand that control of the home does not mean having children who are compliant because their spirits have been crushed or dominated by overly authoritarian parents. Properly trained children are not terrified into subjection. They are given security, peace, and self-discipline by loving parents with a carefully thought-out training plan, and definitely not by ego-driven adults who have to constantly prove that they are in charge.

Prepared parental leaders are at peace, because they are not simply trying to manage and corral out-of-control children. They have confidence because they are in charge, have clearly defined goals, and a plan to achieve those goals. Without confident leadership, parents follow the lead of their children, making theirs a "child-run" home.

WHAT IS A "CHILD-RUN" HOME?

A child-run home is one in which all decisions are made or influenced by the children. Parents in such a home do not feel free to act on decisions they deem wisest, but primarily on what will keep the children happiest. Typically, in a child-run home, parents feel obligated to allow their children a voice in most family matters. The children consequently come to view themselves as part of the parental leadership team. Unfortunately, a child's narcissistic and hedonistic perspective increases when parents continually cater to his preferences and accommodate his misbehavior.

IDENTIFYING A "CHILD-RUN" HOME

Parents in a child-run home will be heard saying things like:

- "I can't make that for dinner at our house. The kids just won't eat it."

- I prepare meals in two batches—one for my husband and me, and one cooked a special way for the kids."

- "Among restaurants, my wife and I enjoy Sizzler, but we never go there . . . the kids prefer the playland at McDonald's."

- "We can't have that family over to the house, their children are so much younger than ours. Ours would not enjoy them."

- "We can't go there, the kids will be bored!"
- "We can never go out. Our children just don't behave for babysitters."
- "We could never take our children into the church service. They wouldn't last."
- "We won't be able to attend. Our little Princess just doesn't do well in those situations."
- "We'll have to find a new church. Junior just doesn't get along with one of the boys in his class."
- "We'll have to change teachers or schools. Little Jane doesn't enjoy Mrs. So-and-so."

Those parents who say, "Junior just refuses to . . . " or "My child just won't put up with . . ." have given up their authority and put their children in charge of their home. They have granted the children veto power and in doing so, must follow their leadership. Needless to say, for those parents who have shared their authority with their children, parenting will be very difficult and unfruitful.

PARENTS SHARE THEIR AUTHORITY WITH THEIR CHILDREN FOR SEVERAL REASONS:

- They may be exercising what some call "democratic parenting." The basis for this approach is that since children are people, with opinions and preferences, they should have rights to influence all decisions affecting them. The error of this kind of thinking is obvious. To grow in maturity, and to be prepared for "real life" (which does not give them a say in everything), children need to learn self-control by submitting themselves to their parents' control. They must learn that what they want does not absolutely have to happen, and that they can endure quite well without expressing their opinion or getting their way. In the first five years of life, which are the most formative, it is critical that children learn that they can survive the "suffering" of not getting what they want. Those early years are the time when they learn to follow, not lead.

- They misunderstand grace. Many well-meaning parents think they are helping their children by not requiring consistent compliance with their leadership. They set up flexible boundaries, believing they are respecting their children's feelings and preferences. Yet, every time parents attempt to exercise authority, but cave in to the resistance of their child, they subtly reward him for bucking authority and they strengthen his will in the process. Those parents, by not exercising their authority, ultimately hinder their children from reaching maturity.

- Some parents are "child-centered" in their child rearing. Instead of helping children curb their narcissistic and hedonistic tendencies, they accidentally strengthen self-absorption by living to give them a happy and fulfilling childhood. These parents make all decisions based on their children's moods and desires. Since they live for their children's happiness, their goal is to minimize the challenges their children might face, and make life as fun and entertaining as possible. Parents of this type strive to please their children, but find them rarely appreciative or satisfied. Such kids are sent the message that they are the center of the universe, so they grow up with an attitude of entitlement and little thankfulness. Child-centered parenting indulges and accommodates children, so they grow up expecting that everything is about them.

- The primary reason that modern parents give away their authority is that they are insecure and crave their children's approval. They try to make their children happy and seek to avoid disappointing them, because they want to be liked. However, their need for their children's love often has the opposite effect—they become despicable to their children. Ultimately, insecure parents become intimidated by their own children, and therefore are hampered in giving strong leadership.

TRAITS OF AN INTIMIDATED PARENT

Insecure parents are like politicians—they need the approval of their constituents, so they say or do whatever they can to maintain popularity. Like someone elected to office, intimidated parents offer very little real leadership, because they are working too hard to keep the constituents happy. Such a parent is certain they are loving their children, because they just want them to be happy. But however much they love them, they do not do for the children that which they believe is best for them.

Insecure parents want to serve children nutritious meals, but often provide junk food, because the kids insist on it. These parents can't afford everything their children want for Christmas, yet they go into debt to buy it all, so they don't have to listen to the complaints later. Intimidated parents are led by their children's whims, passions, and complaints. When children are young and should be learning to follow leadership, parents harm them by following theirs.

Intimidated Parents . . .

- Need their children's approval.

- Dread making their children mad at them.

- Say, in their hearts, "Please don't hate me."

- Conclude most parental commands with, "Okay?"

- Strive to talk their children into obedience by laying out extensive arguments with each command.

- Become exasperated from nagging and trying to persuade children to comply with directions.

- Instead of chastising for rebellious anger, try to diffuse it with distractions or the offering of treats.

- Find themselves trying to gain their children's approval and permission before administering chastisement, by extensive explaining and apologizing for disciplinary actions; to keep their child's affection, they strive to be understood.

- Hastily lavish affection on the child, rubbing their little bottom immediately after a spanking, because they fear their child's rejection.

- Fear rejection after administering chastisement, so offer treats to regain lost affection.

- Allow children to freely express their opinions, complaints, and criticisms regarding family decisions.

THE IMPORTANCE OF HAVING YOUR CHILDREN'S RESPECT

We as adults do not learn well from those we do not respect, whether it is our pastor, our boss, or our spouse. Children, for the same reason, will not submit themselves to our training if we lose their respect. The parents whose home is child-run have already lost their children's respect and must regain it.[6]

TIPS ON REGAINING AUTHORITY AND EARNING YOUR CHILDREN'S RESPECT

I have devoted an entire chapter to the subject of respect, but the topic of parental control necessitates a brief discussion here:

- To gain respect, parents must cause their children to obey their word.

- A parent in charge of the home speaks a command one time, calmly and clearly, and is obeyed. If you continually threaten,

---

6   How do you respect someone with authority who is afraid to exercise it?

but do not follow through with discipline, you will not regain your children's respect, and will only be contemptible to them. For a parent to earn respect, consistent consequences must follow all disobedience.

- Aim primarily for their *respect*—not their *affection.*

- Those parents who *need* their children's love are crippled in their parenting by their own insecurities. Insecure parents seek their child's love and approval to feel good about themselves, so they cannot offer strong leadership. Their efforts to *give* their children firm discipline and training are hampered by their efforts to gain acceptance *from* them. Children unconsciously sense their parents' need for their approval, and enjoy the power it gives them. The relationship between children and insecure parents is marked by extreme disrespect.

- To regain lost respect, authority must be taken completely back, once and for all.

- The parent who shares authority with a child, and then occasionally attempts to take it back and exercise it, will only be resented.

- To restore lost respect, do not permit your child to argue with you, or show you any other expression of dishonor, familiarity, or contempt.

- If you are in the habit of allowing your children to argue with you, you have lost your authority already. You have permitted them to speak to you with the same familiarity they would show a peer, so when you do attempt to exercise authority, they will despise you.

- To gain respect, watch out for the "Camp Counselor Syndrome." Parents who try to be their child's buddy or pal are like the stereotypical camp counselor who gets close to kids, but is not taken too seriously when exercising firm authority. Parents who try to be their child's pal will often find the child resenting it when authority is exercised, illustrating the saying, "familiarity breeds contempt." Single parents, because they have no mate for friendship, are particularly susceptible to this temptation.[7]

- Do not use your size and authority to tease your children. Dads, in particular, struggle with this one. For example, if you hold a child down to tickle him, don't be surprised if you lose his trust and respect when you later try to exercise your authority.

Parents, we must remember *we* are the ones in charge of the home. We owe no apologies for the exercise of our authority. We are not answerable or accountable to our children, and must never seek their approval for our parenting. As long as we send the message that we need approval, we will not succeed in controlling their behavior, they will not gain self-control, and we will fail to develop maturity in them. On top of that, our homes will be marked by increasingly greater stress the older they get.

KEYS TO ESTABLISHING CONTROL

1. Keep your objective in mind—subjection of their will. Never forget that your overall objective of training is to develop maturity in your children, which means your goal is to give them the ability to say "no" to themselves.

2. Require quick obedience. Give instructions one time, calmly and clearly, and require immediate obedience with a good attitude. Bring a consequence if they do not obey.

---

7   Trying to be their "buddy" is not to be confused with winning their hearts by gaining their trust. Children must be motivated by their love for us as well as their respect for our authority. More discussion on this in chapter 17.

3. Teach your children to obey without being told "why."

It is imperative to shape a child's moral reasoning skills by telling him the wisdom behind parental commands, but it is important that children *first* learn to obey whether they understand "why" or not. Children who learn to obey without knowing "why" develop inner controls and submissive hearts that make them open to moral instruction from their parents.

WHY CHILDREN MUST LEARN TO OBEY WITHOUT KNOWING THE REASONS BEHIND THEIR PARENTS' INSTRUCTIONS

In the last fifty years, parents have lost the vision of requiring children to obey them simply because they are the parents. These parents have developed the habit of trying to persuade children into obedience by offering lengthy explanations for every instruction they give. This has resulted in a generation who know little of quick obedience to authority and who habitually challenge every command not only at home, but at school and in the workplace. Children must learn to obey their parents whether they understand "why" or not. Consider the following reasons:

- A chief characteristic of those in authority is that they are not accountable to those under their control. In fact, the first sign that they have lost control is that they feel the need to constantly explain themselves to those they oversee. Our children, therefore, must learn as toddlers that we will not attempt to talk them into obedience, by proving the value of every instruction.

- If you habitually justify your instructions, you will find yourself enduring your child's wrath if you fail to persuade him with your reasoning. Eventually, it will become his "right" to know your reasoning and agree with you before he will obey.

If your goal is to *persuade* your child to obey, then he is not submitting to your authority—he is only doing what is reasonable to him. No self-control is exercised or learned.

WHEN PARENTS SHOULD GIVE CHILDREN REASONS FOR OBEDIENCE

When a child has demonstrated that he can consistently obey without needing to be persuaded to do so, then he is ready to begin learning the wisdom behind parental commands. This means that parents will *occasionally* begin offering him a brief reason for obedience. As he grows and demonstrates he can still obey at the times no reasons are given, he shows himself ready to hear parental wisdom more often.

A parent's goal is to train children to become fully self-governing, motivated toward good behavior not by Mommy's prohibitions, but by well-developed personal values. This will require that parents give wisdom for parental commands much of the time, but not necessarily all of the time. The parent who occasionally offers no reason for obedience to their older children, reinforces the importance of submitting to authority whether reasons are understood or not.

AN EXAMPLE OF APPROPRIATE AND INAPPROPRIATE DIALOGUE WITH OLDER CHILDREN

Appropriate Parental Instructions

"Honey, please play on the other side of the house. The baby is sleeping and you might wake him."

Appropriate Response

"Yes, Mom."

Inappropriate Responses

"But I'll be quiet."

"But I usually play out here and he doesn't wake up."

"But I don't like it in the other side of the house."

"But it's time for him to wake up."

"You never let me have any fun."

Further help on teaching children to respond with respect can be found in chapter 10, "Raising Respectful Children."

GIVING REASONS WITHOUT INVITING ARGUMENTS

Children must be taught to make good decisions in life, but giving brief reasons for obedience does not mean offering *thorough explanations* at the time of the command. Many parents accidentally invite debate from their children by allowing a discussion of their reasoning at the moment obedience is required. Children should not be allowed to question your reasoning at that moment. This policy must be established early in their childhood, because it is difficult to retrain children who have been conditioned to expect a discussion and persuasive reasons for obeying. Children should be allowed to request clarification of parental directions, but not be allowed to engage them in debate.

When parents offer a brief statement of wisdom while giving instructions, children should be referred back to an earlier time of formal family instruction on godliness, or they should know a detailed explanation will come later. For example, the child who is told, "Johnny, please play more quietly. Others are being disturbed by your noise," is merely being reminded of the biblical admonition to "love your neighbor as yourself," and is expected to comply with the insights of his parents. If the situation is new, and Johnny does not understand the logic behind his parents' request, he should be able to respectfully obey and anticipate an explanation later during a parent-initiated time of family instruction.

WHAT ABOUT AN OLDER CHILD WHOSE WILL HAS NEVER BEEN SUBDUED AND HAS NOT BEEN TRAINED TO OBEY HUMBLY?

Many parents reading this book have older children whose wills were not brought into submission when they were young—they are full of themselves and voice their opinions about every command given them. Although they did not learn self-denial during their most formative years, it is not too late for them. Since their root need is to learn to say "no" to themselves, they must go back and learn to obey without discussion. Here's one possible plan:

- After finishing this book, you should approach them and apologize for failing to properly develop within them maturity and prepare them for adulthood.

- Explain how they must learn to humbly accept parental directions without always knowing the reasons why.

- Give them a time period for demonstrating quiet, humble obedience (perhaps six to eight weeks[8]), during which all parental commands will be given without reasons, and no appeals will be considered.

- Tell them they will be required to respond, "Yes, Mom," or "Yes, Dad," to every command, unless it is an emergency. Only then may they make an appeal.

- An emergency is defined as a time when they have no ability to carry out the command, or they know the parent giving the command lacks information which will most certainly affect the command given, i.e., the other parent has given a contradictory command; they have no transportation to go somewhere; there is insufficient food for preparation

---

8   If an eighteen-year-old rebel can learn to answer "Yes, Sir," and make a perfect bunk in the first week of a nine-week military boot camp, a ten-year-old can learn to be respectful in the same amount of time.

of a meal; the detergent box is empty, so clothes cannot be washed, etc.

- Explain to them that if at the end of the time period, they consistently obey quickly and respectfully, then you will begin to give wisdom behind your commands.

- You must make clear to them, however, that when you begin sharing wisdom behind commands, it will not be the same as your former habits, when you allowed debates. The reasons you give will be brief and may not be discussed at the moment of instruction.

- If, at the end of the preset time period, they have not proven they can obey without question, then extend the period, and train them until they have gained self-control.

Keep in mind that as they grow and demonstrate they can submit unquestioningly to authority, you can entrust them with more reasons for obedience.

RESPECTFUL WAYS OF CHANGING A PARENT'S MIND

Although parents must be careful to not invite discussion about every parental command, children who are humble and respectful in their attitude should have the opportunity to appeal parental decisions at times. The key to making an acceptable appeal is the respectful attitude in which it is made. Children must never be allowed to dishonor parents by responding with a raised voice, sass, or angry objection. Parents must be careful not to reward such disrespect by continuing the discussion. If children do not learn early in life to be self-controlled in their communication, they will become belligerent as teenagers and will lack self-restraint in all other relationships. Children should have the opportunity for appeals, but only if they demonstrate honor for their parents. More discussion on respectful appeals in chapter 10.

RESPONDING TO CHILDREN WHO ASK "WHY?"

A fundamental principle of child training is that children should not be permitted to respond continuously to parental commands with "Why?" Two primary reasons:

- It shows resistance to parental authority and delays immediate obedience.

- It is disrespectful in that it is a command to explain. The appropriate responses to any parental directive are: "Yes, Dad," "Sure, Mom," "May I appeal?" or possibly, "May I have your permission to ask why?" but never just, "Why?"

Keep in mind that there is nothing wrong with a child's desire to know his parents' reasoning. Curiosity is natural and children do need their moral values shaped by learning the wisdom behind parental commands. That which is disrespectful, however, is the quick *demand* to know "why?" Such a challenge assumes a parent is accountable to a child. The child who *insists* they be told "why" must not be rewarded by hearing the reason. Respond by requiring that he think of a more respectful way to ask the question. After he does, then explain that you will answer him after he has obeyed.

Remember the biblical account of Job? Throughout his painful trial, he accused God of injustice, challenging His right to permit his suffering. Although God could have explained to Job His reasons for allowing the trial, He never did tell Job "why." He would not honor Job's disrespectful insistence on an answer.[9] Even after Job finally humbled himself and repented of

---

9   Even a righteous person like Job can become disrespectful of authority when he takes his eyes off the Lord and puts them on himself and his problems.

his pride,[10] he received no answer from God. As parents, we must follow God's example and not reward our children's disrespect.

Children who habitually challenge "why" when given a command most likely do so because their parents have offered them a reason for obedience and then allowed dialogue about it. By engaging in debate, parents become exasperated and either attempt to persuade with the logic of the command, or come back with the ever-brilliant response, "Because I said so." Of course *you* said so—they just heard you say it. What you really meant was that they should obey because of your *parental authority*. The problem is that you should establish your authority early on in their life and never have to refer back to it. The very fact that you frequently remind them of your authority reinforces to them that you are not sure of it. Consider your dialogues in light of Proverbs 26:4–5.[11] (More discussion in chapter 6, "Nurturing Children With Discipline.")

CURIOSITY OR AVOIDANCE?

Parents should consider that children usually do not ask "why?" because they desire to grow in wisdom, but because they want to debate their parents' reasoning, and thereby avoid obedience. Those children who respectfully ask the reason for a parental command should have the opportunity to discover their parents' wise reasoning, but *thorough* discussion should usually be permitted only *after* they have obeyed. To always allow discussion before they obey invites them to debate. A good motto to teach them is, "Obey first. Ask questions later."

---

10   Job 42:1–6.

11   Prov. 26:4–5: "Do not answer a fool according to his folly, or you will be like him yourself. Answer a fool according to his folly, or he will be wise in his own eyes."

4

THE FOUR SEASONS OF PARENTING

When I was a boy of fourteen, my father was so ignorant I could hardly stand to have the old man around. But when I got to be twenty-one, I was astonished at how much he had learned in seven years.[1]

The Scriptures describe Christ's followers as children born into God's family, who start off as babes and grow to maturity. From the biblical pattern of Christian discipleship and growth, we can build a loose model for raising children from infancy to adulthood. This will give us an overall view of a parenting plan that will be helpful in formulating a long-range strategy for training our children. The plan incorporates four seasons: *Control, Instruction, Coaching,* and *Friendship.*

---

1   Attributed to Mark Twain (unsubstantiated).

1. CONTROL: AGES 0–4

Jesus taught that the Christian life begins with denying ourselves, taking up our cross, and following him.[2] In other words, our very first baby steps as Christians demonstrate a disregard for our own will and submission of our life to Christ's control.[3] Just as baby Christians yield to the authority of Christ, so also our own children need to start their lives yielding to our authority.

Thus far we have been discussing the first season of parenting—the season of control. Let's review some foundational ideas.

In the first few years of life, because our children are born willful just like us, they must be trained by correction and chastisement to accept an authority outside themselves. It is our responsibility as parents to begin preparing them for real life by teaching them that they are not the center of the universe, and that their personal gratification cannot be the driving force for all those around them. You will observe that from your strong, consistent leadership, they are happiest as *followers*, relieved of the stress of making decisions for themselves and the family. The first several years of life are not the season for them to develop independence and decision-making skills. It is not the season for them to learn to make plans—it is the season of learning to deny "self" and cooperate with Mommy and Daddy's plans. As they submit to our *outer* controls, they will gain *inner* controls.

Some parents will assume that they are with the program because they are geared up to start requiring obedience from their preschoolers. However, establishing control means more than that. To have full control of young children means to take complete responsibility for *directing* their lives. Parents must get the

---

2   Matt. 16:24–26; 10:37–38.

3   Rom. 12:1; Luke 22:42; 14:26–27.

children accustomed to accepting their leadership by making all decisions for them. This means that for the first few years, don't ask them about their preferences. Announce to them what food they will eat, what book they will read, and what clothes they will wear. Of course your three-year-old won't be happy at first. After all, he has been accommodated like royalty, and has come to expect to get his way. As you can imagine, it is best to start this when children are infants, rather than when they are three.

To determine if you are giving full leadership to your young children, listen to yourself. Do you hear yourself making any of the statements listed in the section "Identifying a 'Child-Run' Home"?[4]

Like the believer who bows his head and says, "Yes, Lord," is ready to learn from Jesus,[5] our young children prove their readiness for moral instruction by their consistent submission to us. Therefore, we must spend the first several years of their lives teaching them to say No to themselves and Yes to us. They have many more years to grow in wisdom—the first few years are chiefly for developing self-control. Learning to look to us for leadership gives them the self-discipline they will need to be leaders themselves one day.

2. INSTRUCTION: AGES 4–12

After our children have spent a few years saying, "Yes, Mommy," "Yes, Daddy," and obeying us the first time we speak, they have the foundational ingredient of maturity, and are ready to begin learning wisdom, values, and responsibility. This means that

---

4   Page 34.

5   Luke 14:33; 6:46; Titus 2:12.

we must be conscientious and take time to instruct them about loving God and loving their neighbors as themselves, among other things. It also means that we must no longer make all their decisions for them, but gradually begin to allow them to make personal decisions and live with the consequences of their choices. It's all part of bringing our children to maturity.

If we are procrastinators by nature, we must fight against postponing the instruction of our children. We can put off taking out the trash or paying our taxes, and the consequences won't impact eternity, but if we inadvertently neglect to teach and train the little ones entrusted to us, we may regret it forever. We must remember that maturity is not a natural result of aging—children need to be brought there through discipline and instruction in the Lord.[6] They will not develop the traits of maturity through osmosis or by spending time with other untrained children—it will require a conscious effort on the part of involved parents.[7] What they need from us is not just instruction, but *discipleship*.

Jesus told the apostles not just to sign up members into his Church, but to make disciples of all those who follow him.[8] A disciple is different from a pupil. A pupil is one who is *taught*—a disciple is one who is *trained*. A *pupil* is instructed but may not learn—a *disciple* learns and becomes like his master. We must spend our children's preadolescent years grooming them like disciples,[9] working to instill values within them, so that they will become wise, responsible, and selfless by adolescence. This requires diligence in instruction and modeling as well.

Instructing children is not simply lecturing them when they

---

6   Eph. 6:4.

7   Deut. 6:6–9.

8   Matt. 28:19.

9   Col. 3:16.

have broken a rule and face consequences. Our children certainly need admonishment or correction when they have done wrong, but most are not open to in-depth learning when they are in trouble—they are too defensive and self-preserving at that moment. The best time for learning is at a time separate from the incident. Jesus showed us that the best instruction is not *reactive* but *proactive*. He certainly capitalized on life's examples to teach lessons, but the gospels reveal that He spent most of the time equipping his followers during times set aside for teaching.

Instructing children also does not mean trying to make them wise by giving them multitudes of reasons each time we want them to obey. Our children must learn the wisdom behind our commands, but the moment we need obedience is not the time to do in-depth teaching. Parents who give their children lots of reasons to carry out each command should realize that they have a weak view of their own authority and are attempting to *persuade* children to comply. The more a parent tries to talk a resistant child into obeying, the more a child comes to view himself as an equal to his parent. Argumentative and sassy children usually get that way because parents start the conflict by justifying their instructions. All a young child needs with a command is a simple nugget of wisdom, but this "nugget," if it is a new concept, must be further developed in a time of instruction after they have obeyed or later during devotions.

As Jesus modeled, the most effective discipling occurs during times set aside for instruction. This requires regular times of Bible-based teaching about doctrine and kingdom living. I have never written on the subject of instruction of children, but those who have heard my series "Biblical Insights Into Child Training" know that I devote an entire session to it. I encourage all who have not heard that CD series to get it. We must have a biblical approach to discipling children.

3. COACHING: AGES 12–19

The apostle Paul loved Christ's people like his own children and related differently to different ones, according to their behavior. To the immature, like the Corinthians, he dealt firmly, like a father dealing with small children.[10] To the more mature, like the Thessalonians, he spoke in tender terms,[11] encouraging them as a gentle father[12] and nurturing mother.[13] He was generally not harsh, but came alongside like a *coach*, which should not surprise us, considering he viewed Christians as athletes in a race.[14] We can learn to parent our teens from Paul's parental coaching of the Church.

A study of the book of Proverbs reveals that Solomon also used this approach with his teenage sons. He gave them commandments,[15] but sought to motivate them by reason and concern for natural consequence. He had authority as their father and as the king to both *command* and *threaten* them, but he knew they were young men who needed to choose to do what was right, so he chose to *coach* them. Browbeatings or threats of punishment may seem to keep a teenager in line, but by Solomon's example we have to conclude that they are not as effective as relating to our teens with respect as young adults.

There is much I can say about parenting teens, which I must save for another book, but let me offer just a couple of thoughts on coaching here:

---

10   1 Cor. 3:1–3; 4:15, 21; 6:5; 15:34; 2 Cor. 10:9–11.

11   1 Thess. 1:2–7; 3:6–9.

12   1 Thess. 2:11.

13   1 Thess. 2:7.

14   Acts 20:24; 1 Cor. 9:24–27; Gal. 2:2, 7; 2 Tim. 2:5; 4:7; Heb. 12:1; Phil. 2:16.

15   Prov. 2:1; 3:1; 7:1–2.

1. To coach means we must cease relating to them in a condescending manner, as if they were still young children—we must interact with them respectfully as if they were young adults. Habitual harsh scolding can easily discourage someone who already grieves over his or her failures. Scolding effectively says, "shame on you," focusing their eyes back on themselves in a demoralizing way. Look at it this way—our teens are very young adults—let's treat them like they are. Admonish them the way you would like to be admonished by those who have authority over you. Create disciplinary consequences for misdeeds, but in your tone, relate with them in a way that allows them to keep their adult dignity.

2. We must help our teens identify their behavioral and spiritual goals, and like a coach who believes in an athlete, we must come alongside and encourage them when they fail to achieve their goals. Coaches admonish athletes, so you will have occasion to admonish them, but be careful of always thinking the worst of their motives. Parents who *coach* will find less alienation and greater repentance.

4. FRIENDSHIP: AGE 20+ (OR 16, 17, OR 18+)

Near the end of His ministry, Jesus looked at His disciples and said, "I no longer call you servants, because a servant does not know his master's business. Instead, I have called you friends, for everything that I learned from my Father I have made known to you."[16] Jesus spent more than three years instructing His followers in what the Father had given Him to share. In the beginning, He viewed them as *servants*, but after grooming them in righteousness, He saw them as *friends*. The culmination of discipleship is *friendship*—most parents hope for the same with their children.

---

16   John 15:15.

Our goal in training and discipling our children, is to bring them to maturity. If we are so blessed, they become self-governing and ready for adulthood long before it is time to release them from the home. They will have their own walks with Christ, and will not need us to schedule their daily Bible reading. A well-trained teen will be completely ready for friendship by age twenty, although some are there much younger. When they reach that stage, we will not only have the satisfaction of a job complete, but we will discover ourselves enjoying a growing friendship with them. Not a peer-level friendship characterized by familiarity and impertinence, but one marked by fondness, honor, and respect.

5

METHODS OF INCORRECT DISCIPLINE

In the old days child guidance was something parents were expected to provide and not submit to.[1]

Before we look at the biblical approach to discipline in chapter 6, let us first consider a few unbiblical and fruitless methods of training children. I offer the following examples of incorrect training (methods that guarantee failure), with thanks to my mentor, Rick Fugate.[2]

1. REPEATING INSTRUCTIONS AND MAKING THREATS

Multitudes of parents these days attempt to get cooperation from their children, but remain frustrated because they have to repeat instructions day after day. They frequently hear themselves saying

---

1   *14,000 Quips & Quotes*, E.C. McKenzie, Baker Book House.

2   Adapted from the seminar "What the Bible Says About Child Training," Foundation for Biblical Research, 1996, J. Richard Fugate.

things like, "How many times must I tell you . . . !" (and the kid is thinking, "I don't know, but I'll count.") Repeating parents say things like, "I'm not gonna tell you again!" (And the kid is thinking, "Sure you will. You're not even red in the face yet.") Or parents say, "I've told you a hundred times!" (Which is the whole problem—you've told them multiple times, but with no consequence.) Which catch phrases do you use?

For the parents who only get results when they repeat instructions, I have good news. If your children have the ability to obey after the third or the one hundredth time, *they have the ability to obey.*

Wait—have you got that? They actually have the ability to obey—they are simply waiting for you to be serious about your request. Since you are willing to repeat yourself and not bring a consequence, they aren't motivated to comply.

Your willingness to repeat yourself, albeit with increasing intensity, has actually taught them to ignore you. You have accidentally trained them to disregard your words. You can change this pattern today by announcing to your children that from now on you will only tell them to do something *one time, calmly,* but then you must bring a consequence if they don't obey. You will be astonished how this one practice can transform your home.

Feeling the need to repeat oneself is one of the most frustrating aspects of parenting, yet we must keep in mind that our children are merely doing as they have been trained. There is no basis for our anger at them, since we are the ones administering the faulty training.

SUBTLE SIGNS THAT PARENTS FINALLY MEAN BUSINESS

If you do not require obedience the first time you speak, you force your children to look for signs that you are serious and will finally bring consequences:

You use some catch phrase, such as:

- "I mean it!"
- "Don't you look at me like that!"
- "Do you want a spank?"
- "All right! Now you're gonna get it!"
- "Wait 'til your father gets home!"
- "You keep that up and I'll give you something to cry about!"
- "If I have to come in there, you're really going to get it!" or "If I have to get up . . . !"

Your voice gets harsh, your eyes narrow, and you use their middle name.

You clench your jaw and pronounce your words slowly and precisely.

Your face reaches a familiar shade of red, your eyes bug out, and you slur your words in low guttural sounds. (The children may even be uncertain which language you are speaking.)

Your voice gets so shrill, glass starts to shatter.
That vein in your neck begins to pulsate.

You fly into a rage and begin screaming, "Now you've done it! Are you happy? You've pushed me over the edge!"

CONDITIONING CHILDREN TO RESPOND TO YOUR CALM VOICE

At this point, some parents are possibly thinking, but you don't know my kids, I *have* to raise my voice to them. They *never* respond to gentle and calm speaking.

What you really mean is, "so far they haven't responded to gentle instructions." Fortunately, that is easy to change.

It is a fact of life that people respond to warnings to the degree they believe them. If historically there has been no consequence when you have spoken gently, you have communicated to the children that you should not be believed. Like the little boy who cried "wolf," you have lost credibility with your kids.

Speaking harshly conditions our children to respond only to harshness. The very fact that they respond only to commands given in a harsh or stern tone, means that they know all other commands from us are not to be taken seriously. Fortunately, we can recondition our children by giving all instructions calmly and one time.

REPEATED INSTRUCTIONS ARE *WARNINGS*

If you have not grasped it yet, consider that every time you repeat instructions, you are merely issuing *warnings*. With every warning, your word loses meaning. If your word is meaningless, you've lost the respect necessary for successful training.

- Warnings make you an accomplice to their crimes. By not bringing immediate consequences, you are aiding and abetting them in their disobedience.

- To repeat an instruction is a form of coddling that causes our children to grow dependent on us to remind them of their responsibilities. (Further discussion in chapter 8.)

MAKING THREATS

Ineffective parenting is not only characterized by repeating instructions, but also by *making threats*. Few parents find pleasure in carrying out disciplinary consequences, so fall into the habit of goading their children into compliance by intense notifications of coming trouble. These sweet parents would rather threaten their children than discipline them. After all, an intensely worded threat of impending doom seems so much more peaceful than making a big scene out at the woodshed.

It definitely is *easier* for parents to make threats than to go to the trouble of bringing disciplinary consequences—but note the word "easier." Making threats can be a sign of *lazy* parenting. When we stop everything and go properly deal with children, it sends the message to them that they are worth the trouble. They subconsciously perceive that they are valuable to us.

Besides, the longer we put off dealing with misbehaving children, the angrier we will be when we finally are forced into action. Angry parenting is only damaging.

Examples of making threats:

- "If you don't do such and such, you're going to be in big trouble."

- "You better do what you were told or else!"

- "Do you want a spank?"

- "Want me to get the paddle? Here I go. (Stomp, stomp, stomp). Okay, I'm getting the paddle. Okay, I've got it and I'm coming in now to give you a spank if you've not obeyed yet. Okay?"

- "You want me to count? 1, 2, 3, 4, 5, 6, 7, 8, 8½, 9, 9½, 10. Wow, you juuuust made it."

- Blatant lies. Typical: "Okay, we're leaving without you. Bye, bye." Outrageous: "If you don't behave yourselves, we will leave you here at Disneyland, and they will chain you into "It's a Small World," and you'll be there forever. Where do you think they get all those kids to sing that song? They were naughty ones left behind by their parents."

It is important to note that if your child is asserting his will against yours, causing you to want to issue threats of what is about to happen, he is already in need of discipline. (Further discussion on discipline in the next chapter.)

And let me clarify that a *threat* is different than a *once-in-a-lifetime warning*. When our children are toddlers, we should warn them once about consequences for misbehavior. After that, if we faithfully bring consequences, experience will teach them that they are always to take us seriously. No more need for threats or warnings.

A WORD OF CAUTION: We must not be angry at our children if they are not yet in the habit of obeying us the first time we speak to them. Either they are young and we have not finished their training yet, or we have accidentally trained them to disobey, and it will require self-discipline on our part to break our habit of repeating instructions. Either way, we must be patient—*they are still in training!*

2. BRIBING FOR OBEDIENCE

The difference between a bribe and a reward is that *bribes* are given to motivate behavior that should be mandatory. It is an effort by one *without* power to buy a favor from the one *with* power. *Rewards*, on the other hand, are typically given to reinforce learned skills, good habits, or to give encouragement for the accomplishment of a non-moral task. *Moral* behavior may also be rewarded, but such rewards are not offered in advance because they would act as bribes for good behavior—they are best given without prior warning, and only occasionally. (For more understanding of *rewards*, see Rewards vs. Consequences, page 93).

The parent who is unaware of his authority sometimes resorts to offering bribes to his children to evoke obedience:

- "We will pay you a dollar now and another one when we return, if we get a good report from the babysitter."
- "If you behave in the grocery cart, I'll get you a treat when we check out."
- "If you get into bed for your nap, I'll read your favorite story."
- "You may have cake for dessert if you eat your vegetables first."
- "If you sit still and smile for the photographer, I'll buy you ice cream when we get done. So please sit still! It'll be Baskin-Robbins. Okay, honey?"

Bribing children tells them:

- that your word is insufficient motivation to obey;
- that they are in charge and you are not;
- that you are at their mercy; and
- that you are not worthy of their respect.

Parents seeking to eliminate bribing from their training must be careful not to eliminate the reward of verbal praise and affirmation for good behavior.

Remember Solomon's wisdom: " . . . a bribe corrupts the heart."[3] We undermine our own efforts to shape our children's hearts if we corrupt them.

---

3   Eccles. 7:7.

3. ALLOWING EXCUSES

Children must learn as a basic rule that there are no good reasons for disobedience (except in the case of an emergency, of course). When confronted with their defiance, they should not be permitted to offer an excuse. If trained well, it might not even enter their minds to offer a justification.

The parent who allows excuses for disobedience permits a child to avoid the consequences of his actions, inadvertently encouraging misbehavior.

A child whose excuses are routinely accepted develops a "victim" mentality, eventually believing that nothing is ever his fault.

Parents who do not want to think badly of their children may make up an excuse for them before they even investigate a problem, i.e.,

- They get into trouble at school and you automatically believe their story that their teacher is out to get them.

- Before they have a chance to offer an excuse, you presume their innocence and suggest to them an alibi.

The parent who confronts a child for misbehavior and immediately asks, "Why did you do it?" sends the message that if a good enough reason can be offered, punishment may be avoided.

A parent should first establish a child's guilt and have him accept responsibility, and then find out the reason why. (Parents will need to determine if the action was intentional or accidental, so that they can set an appropriate consequence. Further discussion in the next chapter.)

Upon confrontation, a child should be permitted to respectfully state that his actions were of an emergency nature, i.e.,

- "Yes, I pushed my sister, but I didn't mean to hurt her. She was about to be run over by a car, so I tried to push her out of the way."

- "Yes, I got out of bed, but little Jimmy's arm was caught in his crib."

- "Yes, Dad, I interrupted you, and I am sorry for that, but Mom is out in the driveway, leaving in the car, and needs to know if you still want something at the store."

Parents Accept Excuses Because . . .

- We put ourselves in our children's place, and know we would want mercy if it were us.

- We think we are too busy to stop and bring proper discipline.

- We are deceived about our children's nature and fall prey to their manipulation.

- We want to believe the best of our children, so are more than willing to allow them to cast the blame or shirk responsibility.

- We do not know who to believe in a dispute, and literally do not know what to do, so we accept an excuse and send the children off with just a warning.

- We hate conflict, and accepting an excuse is the easiest way to settle a problem.

- We are lazy, and choose our own comfort over our children's needs.

4. TRICKING OR MANIPULATING

Since the goal of child training is to help a child learn to subdue his self-will, parents must take every opportunity to subdue it when it manifests itself. Tricking a child may manipulate him into cooperating, but his will is not subdued in the process. One day he will be too smart to trick, and his parents will have a smart, strong-willed child on their hands, who resists their best parenting efforts.

Examples of Tricking a Child:

- When your authority is not sufficient to motivate your child to pick up their toys, you make a game of it, so that their desire for fun will gain their cooperation.

- When they will not obey your specific direction to go into their room for a nap, you become animated, playful, and silly, to make the walk to their room look like a lot of fun.

- When a child does not want to go outside to play, you give him two choices, i.e., "Do you want to walk outside or do you want me to carry you out?" (He should be made to walk out under his own power in obedience to your word, and not tricked into compliance.)

- Instead of giving them a direct order to go to bed, manipulate them by saying, "Which do you want to take with you to bed right now—the teddy bear or the doll?" Since they don't recall agreeing to go to bed, they become confused, so you take advantage of their confused state and put them quickly in bed with both the doll and the bear.

- When they will not cooperate, you create a contest to gain compliance, i.e., challenging them to get their room clean within a time limit. (This is not to discourage teaching them to set time limits for projects.)

5. DISTRACTING

Distracting children does not shape their will at all. It only diffuses the tension of the moment.

Distracting may be a quick way to settle down a distraught or angry child, but it cannot be a substitute for discipline that will subdue the will. For example:

- A three-year-old who is throwing a fit may forget that he was upset if an animated parent points out the window and exclaims, "What could that be?" No matter how calming the effect of the distraction is, it does not subdue his will and should not be a substitute for chastisement.

- Angry children may be easily calmed by the offering of a toy or a treat in the midst of their distress, but that toy does not serve to subdue their will. It will, in fact, reward them for their behavior and encourage it in the future.

The only time distraction might be used is in a public setting where you are trapped in your seat and others are being disturbed by your child's anxiety, i.e., on a plane, a bus, a submarine, etc. Whenever possible, an unruly child should be taken somewhere private and disciplined, where others will not be disturbed. The defense against being faced with such a situation is to train the child beforehand in the privacy of your home.

6

NURTURING CHILDREN WITH DISCIPLINE

No discipline seems pleasant at the time, but painful. Later on,
however, it produces a harvest of righteousness and peace for
those who have been trained by it.

—Hebrews 12:11

One of the most painful aspects of parenting is the administering of discipline. When we were young, our parents told us, "This hurts me more than it hurts you," but we didn't believe it—until we became parents ourselves. Now we understand it—and we hate it—but we must do it!

The reason so many parents hate discipline is not just because they do not like to see their children cry, but because they are not 100 percent confident they are doing the right thing. Discipline is often stressful for them, because they are plagued by doubts, fears, and guilt.

Fortunately, God has given us in the Scriptures all the basic principles for determining when discipline is warranted and how to administer it. The parent who understands and applies these principles will find peace both in his heart and in his home.

WHAT IS GOD'S METHOD FOR DISCIPLINE?

Fathers, do not exasperate your children; instead, bring them
up in the training and instruction of the Lord. (Ephesians 6:4)

According to Ephesians 6:4, children are brought to maturity
by *training* and *instruction* in the Lord. The Greek word for
training is *paideia*, which means *disciplinary education by correction, chastening, or punishment*. God's method for child training
or "disciplinary education" then involves elements of *correction,
chastisement*, and *punishment*.

CORRECTION communicates the idea of *rectifying* something wrong, confronting a misbehaving child for the purpose of *making things right*. Correction is the foundation of
training.

CHASTISEMENT is the training of a child toward proper
behavior by bringing negative consequences in response to
defiant actions or attitudes. It is negative reinforcement by
means of swats with a rod.

It is important to note that chastisement is not *atonement*. A
spanking does not cause a child to *pay* for his misdeeds. Chastening is simply a form of negative reinforcement that motivates
a child not to repeat an action or attitude.

PUNISHMENT is akin to chastisement and involves
bringing natural consequences for misbehavior. It is used in
response to *thoughtless disobedience.*

WHAT IS THE DIFFERENCE BETWEEN THOUGHTLESS DISOBEDIENCE AND REBELLION?

Under Israelite Law, God distinguished two types of crimes—

intentional and *accidental*. Each had a different penalty. For example, Numbers 35:11–28 tells us that if one man murdered another, he was to be executed—life for life. However, if a man was irresponsible and killed another by accident, he was free to flee to a "city of refuge," where he and his family had to take up residence until the presiding high priest died. The willful murderer *intentionally*[1] violated the law, so suffered an equally severe physical consequence—death. The other *accidentally* violated the law, but still had to endure a consequence for his irresponsibility. Two different crimes—two proportionate penalties.

Biblical discipline of children follows the example God established in Jewish civil law. When a child *willfully* defies his parents and does wrong, he is in rebellion against their authority and must be chastised. If he disobeys them *thoughtlessly*, he is guilty of accidental misbehavior, and must receive a related consequence as a penalty.

The Two Types of Misbehavior:

- Rebellion—willful defiance of authority. It is a condition of heart that says, "I do not accept your authority to make a decision in my life."

- Thoughtless disobedience—accidental misbehavior as a result of a lack of skill or personal discipline.

HOW DOES THE BIBLE SAY TO CHASTISE FOR REBELLION?

The Scriptures make it clear that chastisement is God's proper consequence for rebellion in children. Consider the following passage from Proverbs:

---

1   Num. 35:20.

> Do not withhold chastisement from your children; if you *smite them with a rod*, they will not die. If you *smite them with the rod*, you will save their souls from hell. (Proverbs 23:13–14, emphasis mine)

God tells parents that they are not to withhold spankings from their children, for they help accomplish a soul-saving work.

The Hebrew word for smite is *nakah*, which means "to strike or swat." Parents are clearly instructed that they should train their children, spanking them on the bottom with an implement for chastisement.

It is important to note that according to the Scriptures, spankings are to be administered not with the *hand*, but with the *rod*. The Hebrew word for rod is *shebet*, which means a twig or switch. It is not a heavy implement that may bruise the skin, but a light one that will simply sting. The hand by itself is to be avoided, because it can cause bruising. Besides, those parents who use their hand will notice that their child will be unable to distinguish when he is being reached for in tenderness or in discipline—he will flinch whenever you reach for him.

Throughout the book of Proverbs, God emphasizes the value of the rod in firm discipline.

> Folly is bound up in the heart of a child, but *the rod of discipline will drive it* far from him. (Proverbs 22:15)

> The *rod of correction imparts wisdom*, but a child left to himself disgraces his mother. (Proverbs 29:15)

As we established in the introduction, the Hebrew words translated as "folly" or "foolishness"—*keciyl* and *'ivveleth*—do not mean childish immaturity or silliness, but rather *deviousness, defiance,* and *rebellion.* The root meaning of *keciyl* is "fat," hence to be foolish is to be fat or "bloated with oneself." The rod is God's chosen means of subduing the self-will and rebellion that resides in every child. It is a quick, simple way of teaching obedience. Chastisement is over quickly, the pain soon forgotten, but the impact is lasting. The negative consequence of pain conditions a child to say "no" to himself and thereby helping develop the self-discipline necessary for maturity.

"BUT I LOVE MY CHILDREN TOO MUCH TO SPANK THEM."

He who *spares the rod* hates his son, but he who loves him is careful to discipline him. (Proverbs 13:24)

Chasten thy son while there is hope, and let not thy soul spare for his crying. (Proverbs 19:18, KJV)

Spanking is not easy for most parents, because it brings grief to the very children they naturally want to comfort. Knowing the protective nature He gave us as parents, God warns that allowing soft feelings to inhibit spanking is tantamount to *hating* our children.[2] This only makes sense, since depriving children of what is good and necessary for their moral development will be doing them harm. The problem is that some parents do not spank their children, because they want to spare *themselves* the heartache of watching their children cry, or because they fear their child's rejection.

It is not a healthy love that causes a parent to protect children from experiencing any discomfort or pain in life. In fact, it is often a self-serving love that makes parents refrain from spanking,

---

2   Prov. 13:24.

or causes them to mete out soft disciplines and indulge their children. That kind of parental "kindness" is harmful.

For example, some children fear dentists. For them, just the thought of a dental appointment evokes panic. The overly compassionate parents, who succumb to their child's fears, harm him when they allow him to grow up without dental care. The same parents may even exempt their child from eating "yucky" foods like vegetables, and allow him to eat a steady diet of junk food. The Bible says that those parents actively "hate" their child by depriving him of what is good for him.

True compassion causes parents to ignore their own feelings of anguish at seeing their child's tears, and do what will be best for them in the long run. The parents who withhold the rod may do so out of a desire to spare *themselves* distress and avoid their child's rejection. Any parents who consistently spank their children will testify that it requires selfless love to die to themselves and do what is right for their children. Consider also Proverbs 3:11–12:

> My son, despise not the chastening of the LORD; neither be weary of his correction: For whom the LORD loveth he correcteth; even as a father the son in whom he delighteth. (KJV)

God says that a father who loves and delights in his children will be faithful to discipline them. A significant evidence of God's love for us is His discipline. Consider also Hebrews 12:5–9:

> And ye have forgotten the exhortation which speaketh unto you as unto children, My son, despise not thou the chastening of the Lord, nor faint when thou art rebuked of him: For *whom the Lord loveth he chasteneth*, and *scourgeth* [spanks] every son whom he receiveth. If ye endure chastening, God dealeth with you as with sons; for what son is he whom the father chasteneth not? But if ye be without chastisement, whereof all are partakers, then are ye bastards, and not sons. Furthermore we have had

fathers of our flesh which corrected us, and we gave them reverence: shall we not much rather be in subjection unto the Father of spirits, and live? (emphasis mine, KJV)

God says in verses six to eight that the proof of parents' love is their willingness to spank their children, and that a child who is not spanked can hardly be called a son or daughter.

God, in His love, has determined that suffering hardship is part of the maturing process for all believers,[3] we therefore can trust His brilliance when He tells us that our children learn self-discipline through the discipline imposed by spanking.

The society that does away with corporal punishment will raise undisciplined, self-consumed young people, who lack the security that comes from being required to stay within firm limits. Sweden and Denmark, famous for their prostitution, drugs, and child pornography, are the world's first countries to have outlawed spanking. Not surprisingly, within two decades after they outlawed spanking, they had the highest teen suicide rates in the world. Eliminating the rod is not a sign of a civilized society, but of one in moral decline.

WHAT IS THE DIFFERENCE BETWEEN CHASTISEMENT AND CHILD ABUSE?

Among some parents there is great fear today that spanking is abusive, and causes emotional harm, or may breed violence. This concern is understandable, considering how we love our children. Fortunately, biblical chastisement bears good fruit, but unfortunately, not everyone follows God's guidelines. Consider the differences between loving, biblical chastisement and child abuse:

---

3   Rom. 5:3–5; James 1:2–4; Zech. 13:9; 1 Pet. 1:6–7; 4:1; Heb. 12:7, 10, 11.

- *Chastisement* is a calm, controlled spanking on the bottom.

- *Abuse* is an angry, out-of-control beating, which may fall on the bottom or anywhere on the body. Such abusive chastisement may correct the misbehavior, but that child is not truly humbled—just terrorized into submission.

- *Chastisement* uses a lightweight rod on the bottom.

- *Abuse* shakes the body or pummels it with hands or any weapon handy.

- *Chastisement* is a planned action of love.

- *Abuse* is a reaction of anger. It is the venting of parental frustration, and feeds violence in children, causing them to vent their anger violently on others. (Young ones raised with loving chastisement are typically the least violent among children, because they are self-restrained, are not ruled by their anger, and have been trained to behave kindly toward all.)

- *Chastisement* is done after the first offense, while the parent is still calm.

- *Abuse* results when parents do not bring swift chastisement, but wait for the child's continued rebellion to make them angry enough to respond. Spanking is incorrectly used if it is a last resort rather than the first response for rebellion.

- *Chastisement* is loving and constructive.

- *Abuse* consists of hurtful, demeaning verbal attacks, which may accompany chastisement, but are often a substitute.

- *Chastisement* draws a parent and child together.

- *Abuse* alienates children from their parents.

HOW TO TELL WHEN A TIME OF CHASTISEMENT IS COMPLETED

Many parents implement chastisement with their children, but are frustrated, because it does not seem to subdue their wills.

The most common reason for this is *incomplete chastisement*—it is administered as discipline for rebellion, but is ended before its goals have been accomplished.

What Are the Goals of Chastisement?

1. To cause children to be humble before their parents' authority.

2. To cause them to take responsibility for what they have done.

3. To cause them to submit to the consequences of their actions.

Signs of Unbroken Rebellion after a Time of Chastisement

- No obvious sign of brokenness or humility.

- Unwilling to admit fault and take responsibility for actions. Still blaming others or making excuses for misbehavior. Uses one of the defense mechanisms listed in chapter 10.

- Wallows in self-pity; maintains a "victim" mentality.

- Kicks or struggles the entire time of chastisement, never submitting to the discipline. (Applies primarily to older children. Very young children may not hold still simply because they are not used to spankings.)

- Refuses to hug the disciplining parent.

- Cries out for the non-disciplining parent; i.e., if Daddy administers the discipline, they might call for Mommy.

- Extended or extra loud crying (venting *anger*—not pain or sorrow).

- Blatantly angry: threatens to leave home, curses parent, sassy attitude, throws things, grumbles, storms around the house, etc.

- Tries to make parents feel guilty by sulking or pouting, or accusing them of improper discipline, i.e., "You spanked me in the wrong place."

- Issues taunts like, "You're mean" or "I hate you" or "That didn't hurt" or "I can't wait 'til I'm old enough to move out!"

- Expresses no remorse to God in prayer, and refuses to ask forgiveness of those they offended.

The chastisement is not over until a child is humble and has taken responsibility for his actions. It is only complete when his will is submitted to his parents. If after a time of chastisement a child lacks proper humility, the chastisement obviously did not work, and should be repeated a second time. I rarely hear of any parent needing to administer a third set.[4]

Many parents battle strong-willed, defiant teenagers, because they never successfully completed a time of chastisement in the preadolescent years. Each incomplete time of chastisement served only to challenge, but not defeat their wills, making them stronger and stronger. By accident, some parents create super-strong-willed teens.

Parents who begin implementing chastisement when their children are toddlers, and properly complete each session, generally discover that their wills are completely subdued by the time they are four to five years old. Many testify that only occasional chastenings are required after that age.

---

4   Occasionally I do hear of a child who may not show his humility immediately after chastisement. Such a child, the parents tell me, finds humility when left alone to calm down for a few minutes following chastisement.

BEHAVIOR DURING CHASTISEMENT THAT SHOULD NOT BE ALLOWED, AND MERITS EXTRA DISCIPLINE

It is important during chastisement that our children accept our authority and submit themselves to the discipline we have determined they need. The following actions indicate resistance to your authority:

- Running away from you;

- Moving away from the rod;

- Kicking and struggling;

- Putting their hand in front of their bottom;

- Screaming at you;

- Pleading for mercy; making vehement promises of repentance;

- Requesting limited number of swats;

- Extra loud, angry crying;

- Lying; making excuses; trying to get out of trouble; casting blame; and

- Guilt projection; threatening you; accusing you of improper discipline.

HOW TO KNOW WHICH BEHAVIOR OR ATTITUDE MERITS CHASTISEMENT

Any child who *knowingly or willfully disobeys* is in rebellion and needs chastisement.

Keep in mind that it is not the significant *effect* of the rebellious action that merits the rod—it is the rebellion itself, i.e., it is not that they woke the baby up when they went into the off-limits room—it is the fact that they entered it in direct disobedience to your word. It is not the fact that they only took a crumb of cake after they were told not to touch it—it is that they *intentionally* disobeyed you.

HOW TO IDENTIFY REBELLION[5]

A rebellious child is one . . .

- whose actions or attitude are in direct defiance of parental authority;
- who asserts his will against the will of his parents; and
- who resists his parents' efforts to direct his life.

The attitude of a defiant child says, "I do not accept your authority to make decisions in my life."

Active Rebellion

1. Knowingly disobeying—*Active Rebellion*

   - Willful, conscious disobedience to commands or established rules.

   - Examples: "Come here, Junior," and he doesn't budge. "Stay in bed, Mary!" and she gets up. "Don't wear that, Terry!" and she wears it.

2. Defiant verbal resistance—*Active Rebellion*

   - Any form of sass or backtalk. (See chapter 9.)

   - Intentions to disobey are announced by saying, "No!" Some offer a more blatantly disrespectful phrase of defiance, such as: "Drop dead," "Forget you," "Get a life," or "Whatever," etc.

---

5   Adapted, with additions, from Rick Fugate's, "What the Bible Says About Child Training."

- Will not accept parents' authority to make a decision. Refuses to take "no" for an answer.

- After receiving parent's decision, voices opinions relentlessly, even after instructed that the discussion is over.

- Fostered by parents who cave in to verbal resistance.

3. Hitting parents—*Active Rebellion*

- Feel free to vent their anger. Toddlers may slap, bite, or kick; older children may spit; teens may use their size and strength to cause serious injury.

4. Throwing temper tantrums—*Active Rebellion*

- Pitching a fit because their will has been thwarted.

- Toddlers may hold their breath, go stiff, go limp, cry uncontrollably, or fall down and pound their fists on the floor.

- Children of any age may stomp their feet, scream, yell, throw or hit things, stare and glare, slam doors, etc.

5. Ignoring instructions—*Active Rebellion*

- After receiving parental instruction, they continue to do as they please, as if they had never been spoken to.

- When receiving a tap under the table or a "look" from their parent that obviously says, "Knock it off," they look away or pretend they received no communication. (Parents blind to this form of rebellion will allow a child to not answer, perhaps even excusing their misbehavior as fatigue or mood.)

6. Resisting a parent-initiated action—*Active Rebellion*

- A parent chooses to initiate an action requiring their child's involvement, but the child refuses to cooperate.

- The child moves their shoulder away when a parent reaches out to touch or embrace him.

- Walking along, a parent reaches down and takes their child's hand and the child attempts to pull it away, perhaps continuing to tug until the parent lets go. (If the child is in pain because the blood in their hand has drained to their shoulder, and gangrene is setting in, they should be able to respectfully ask to have their hand back.)

- After being placed on their parent's lap, they attempt to get off. They should be permitted to respectfully ask to get down, but only after the parent is satisfied that they are willing to remain.

- While being held in their parent's arms, a toddler struggles to get down.

- The child goes limp or runs away when being ushered down the street.

- You reach for something in their hand and they hold onto it or pull it away. (They must be made to place the object in your hand. Do not grab or force from them something, unless it is a dangerous item, i.e., knife, match, power tool, razor, etc.)

- After being placed in the highchair, a toddler arches his back and strains against the seat belt.

- Undoes something a parent has done, i.e., turns the stereo volume back up after the parent has turned it down; turns a light back on after the parent has turned it off; retrieves something after parent has put it away.

Passive Rebellion

Rebellion that is passive in expression tends to be less conscious and premeditated than active rebellion. It is more of a rebellious reaction than a planned action. Those passively rebellious are often unaware of their defiance, requiring parents to work harder to expose to them their rebellion.

1. Consistent forgetfulness—*Passive rebellion*

   - Common to children is occasional forgetfulness. Consistent forgetfulness, however, is a form of rebellion.

   - When they can remember to set their alarm and dress themselves for soccer practice, but habitually forget to take out the garbage, they are demonstrating they can be capable when they choose to be. They just need greater motivation.

   - Remembers the entire prime-time TV schedule, or never misses their favorite radio show, but always forgets to do their homework or make their bed.

   - They remember all that is important to them.

2. External obedience with a bad attitude—*Passive rebellion*

   - Obeys outwardly, but sends a defiant message: sulking, grumbling, whining, pouting, angry door slamming, glaring, silence, rough treatment of others or objects, etc.

   - They will obey, because they have to, but they will make you miserable.

   - They cooperate with your directions, but talk, complain, or whine about it the entire time, i.e., the three-year-old who lets his mother shower him, but is permitted to complain throughout the shower: "But I don't want a shower. I don't want a shower."

3. Obeying only on own terms—*Passive rebellion*

- Does not come exactly when called; walks slowly.

- Postpones obedience to show who is boss.

- Does just one more after being told to stop.

- Dictates to parent when they will obey: "I'm getting a drink first," or "I'll be there in a minute."

4. Doing *what* is required, but not *how* it should be done—*Passive rebellion*

- Does chores, but not by parents' established standards, i.e., dishes are not quite clean, bed is not made properly, bedroom is not in order as required.

- You direct them to sit in their high chair and they squat.

- Parents foster rebellion when they decide that rather than fight them, they will settle for partial obedience.

5. Walking away while being spoken to—*Passive rebellion*

- Leaves the room while parent is in mid-sentence or during a pause between sentences.

- Keeps inching his way to the door before he's been dismissed. (Considered *passive* rebellion, because children are often unaware they are doing this.)

6. Lying to escape discipline—*Passive rebellion*

- Premeditated lying is active rebellion, but reactively lying to escape discipline may be so unconsciously done that it qualifies as *passive*.

- Many parents just expect their children to lie to get out of trouble, so neglect to chastise for it. It is important to chastise extra for this form of rebellion.

- To train children to tell the truth about a misdeed, I suggest the following: When they start to tell a lie, announce to them that telling a lie will double the swats for their misdeed (instead of three swats, they will receive six). Let them know that the temptation to lie is understandable, but that they may stop and say the truth, without penalty.

7. Violating unspoken, but understood rules—*Passive rebellion*

- Although some rules are never spelled out, and some behaviors are never specifically prohibited, our children still know better. They intentionally disregard what they know will please you. What gives them away when they are caught is behavior that suggests a violated conscience.

- They must do some justifying in their minds, i.e., Johnny takes Dad's power tool out of the garage to show his friends, knowing it would displease his parents, but justifies it to himself, saying, "Dad lets me use it sometimes." Yet, he jumps and hides the tool when Mom walks up to them.

- Some children grant themselves permission to change an established house rule, because on one occasion their dad saw them violating it, but did not say anything. Their dad's inattention to what they were doing did not mean the rule had changed, and they know that, but they conveniently took his silence as permission.

- The toddler who is caught in the bathroom unrolling the toilet paper, may not have been specifically forbidden to unroll the tissue, but the tears he sheds, and the haste with which he continues his deed as he sees his mother approaching, verify that he knows he is doing wrong.

ARE THERE ALTERNATIVES TO CHASTISEMENT?

As I stated in the preface, I do not want to promote a cookie-cutter approach to parenting. Not all children are the same and neither is every circumstance, so we mustn't use an oversimplified formula for devising responses to all of our children's behavior. Generally, we are to use chastisement to train the willfulness out of our children, especially our very young children. Since the wisdom of the Word is so clear, we must avoid hunting for "creative alternatives" to chastisement, even if we are uncomfortable with the idea of it.

However, as we follow the Bible and take heed to all of its principles, we must remember that there is latitude in applying its wisdom. The Proverbs passages are presented not as inflexible moral commands like "do not murder" or "do not commit adultery," but as generally wise guidelines for life. If we have an adopted child that suffered abuse in a foreign orphanage, they may be unresponsive to typical chastisement. It is possible that an alternative disciplinary consequence may subdue their will or draw them out of their emotionally protected (RAD)[6] condition. Or it is possible that your total love and acceptance may be incentive enough to draw them out of themselves. My point is that we must use our brains if we see that chastisement is not having the desired effect. Let us not continue to chastise a child that needs something else.

If your child has no special needs, and is typically obedient, but occasionally manifests defiance out-of-character, then it also might be the time to evaluate the necessity of chastisement for that incident. Before doing anything, a parent should determine: Is this defiance characteristic of my child, or might there be some-

---

6   Reactive Attachment Disorder—a personality condition that can develop in children who have been victimized by early childhood abuse or trauma.

thing happening at a deeper level that is causing this rebellion?

Here are a few of things I have found that can cause a well-behaved child to rebel, and should be dealt with at a heart level rather than by spanking:

Provoked to Violence: It is possible that your otherwise well-mannered son hit his little sister because her constant antagonism finally wore him down. A violent response breaks the family rule about kindness and love, but it will be better in this circumstance to patch up the relationship between them than to just spank him for hitting, particularly if he is over five years of age. When God warns parents about exasperating their children and making them lose heart[7] it was for situations just like this.

Broken Relationship: It has been said that rules without relationship is a recipe for disaster. In families, I have found that when a trust relationship is broken or completely absent between child and parent, the child ceases to welcome parental wisdom or benefit from any discipline. Before exacerbating the problem with automatic spankings, I would recommend that a parent reevaluate their trust relationship with their child. Is it possible that your ten-year-old's actions were not a result of hardened rebellion against good rules, but were against the parent who was exasperating him or causing him heart pain? If the rebellion was caused because your child has become exasperated by you, it would be worth evaluating what you may have been doing in your parenting. At a time like that, it would be good to reread chapter 15 on how we exasperate children.

---

7   "Fathers, do not exasperate your children, that they may not lose heart." Col. 3:21; Eph. 6:4.

Heart of Pain: Our children, whether they are seven or seventeen, can wrestle with stress and heartache just as we can. When they have had a hard day they must learn that they cannot take out their anger on their possessions or on other people. However, a parent must determine—will a spank cure their frustration or will compassion from an understanding parent meet a deeper need? If they have taken out their anger on possessions or people, at the very least they need to rectify any damage done. They definitely must learn that out-of-control behavior is never acceptable.

RESPONDING TO REBELLION WITH THREATS
(The Danger of Threatening to Spank)

In the previous chapter, I discussed the importance of not threatening impending consequences. A deep understanding of this is so important that I am continuing that discussion here.

Children must learn early on that it is the authority of a parent's word that they must heed, and that spankings will always be merited by willful defiance of that word. The parent who makes that clear to a young child and then proceeds throughout their childhood to regularly warn of each impending spank, accidentally sends the message that their word is not to be taken seriously. Their warnings may succeed in curtailing immediate misbehavior, but their child will learn to disrespect their word—and them.

Parents usually offer these warnings because they hope to correct rebellion without resorting to spanking. However, the child who is asserting his will against his parents is already in need of chastisement. The constant threats and reminders of impending spanks are blatant efforts to *persuade* a child to cease from misbehavior, and will not subdue the will.

THE CLEAR RULE: Tell a child a few times early in his life that he must be absolutely obedient to your word. After that, he must be held accountable to abide by all parental commands and should expect the pre-established consequences for violations, without further warnings.

HOW TO IDENTIFY THOUGHTLESS DISOBEDIENCE

There is a huge difference between a child that is guilty of rebellion and needs chastisement, and one that is guilty of thoughtless disobedience and needs to make restitution.

In its basic core, thoughtless disobedience . . .

- is any accidental violation of a rule or parental command.

- is not willful or defiant, nor is it planned or premeditated.

- is typically an impulsive, careless, or irresponsible action, or an honest mistake.[8]

- is an action which merits correction and a punitive consequence.

There is a vast difference between the boy who spills his milk out of clumsiness and the boy who has the skill to aim it at his sister. They both need a consequence, but not the same one.

DISCIPLINE OF THOUGHTLESS DISOBEDIENCE

The most effective consequences for acts of thoughtless disobedience are those in which the penalty is related to the crime. In this way, the consequence reinforces the lesson that needs to be learned.

---

8   An honest mistake might be forgetting to carry out instructions or breaking a lamp from clumsiness.

Less effective disciplines are those which have nothing to do with the misdeed, i.e., when a child thoughtlessly leaves his bike out for the second time, what will teach him to be more responsible with his possessions? Will "grounding" him teach him to put his bike away? Will a "time out"? Sitting him in the corner? Fining him? Assigning him ten pages of sentences? None of these will be as effective as creating a consequence which relates directly to his failure.

The child who leaves his bike out has proven himself *irresponsible* with a personal possession—he needs to learn *responsibility*. A consequence that might teach him to be more responsible with his bike would be the loss of it for a time. Every time he wants to use it, but can't, he is reminded of his need to be more responsible with his bike. Plus, *he*—not Dad—will need to spend time removing the rust from the bike frame, which resulted from leaving the bike out in the evening dew.

What does a parent do about a child who consistently forgets to close the front door or always slams it? Might I suggest that you have him practice entering the house and closing the door gently behind him for five minutes. And keep in mind that his failings were not intentional and he doesn't need your anger.

A FEW TYPICAL CONSEQUENCES AND PRINCIPLES TO CONSIDER

1. Loss of privileges. Parents must realize that most of what their children are allowed to do or to have is a *privilege*—not a *right*. Privileges should be revoked for those who prove themselves irresponsible. It is very important that the children be told in advance the possible discipline they will bring upon themselves.

   - Toys or clothes that are repeatedly left out may be taken away—permanently or for a period of time.

- If older children are lazy or irresponsible in work, they repeat the chore, get extra jobs, or miss the next meal.[9] They are not being punished—they are just honing their skills.

- Declare to your children that they must complete their chores before they may leave for recreational outings. If it is time for them to leave for an outing, but you determine they were irresponsible,[10] so did not complete their chores, they must not be permitted to go until they are done. If a sports team has to compete without them,[11] they must learn the lesson that personal irresponsibility can hurt others. Most children who incur this kind of penalty rarely repeat the same irresponsibility a second time.

- If they are near the age for a driver's license, emphasize to them that driving is a privilege for those who prove themselves responsible. Postpone the date they may apply for their license by one month every time they manifest significant irresponsibility.

- If dinner is eaten too slowly or complained about, declare dinner over, take it away, and give it to them for breakfast the next morning. (Parents testify that this is one of the most effective disciplines they have ever tried.)

- If the family is at a restaurant and Dad orders everyone the pancake special or the family-sized spaghetti bowl, but the children are unthankful for his gift, cancel their order and allow them only water to drink. (Sounds harsh, but parents testify that after applying

---

9   2 Thess. 3:10b " . . . if anyone will not work, neither let him eat."

10   Only if their uncompleted tasks were because of irresponsibility, and not because you gave them too much to do.

11   If it is not the championship game.

this discipline just once with one child, the others all learn and behave gratefully the rest of their lives. It is important they be forewarned of this penalty.)

- If they nag or "push" you to do something for them, bringing it up after they have been instructed to drop the subject, they automatically lose it, even if you were already intending to give it to them.

- If they speak to you with disrespect, for a period of time they lose the privilege of speaking about what was on their mind.

2. Rectifying the damage done:

- Restitution—paying the cost of replacing items lost or broken. Children too young to have money should travel with you to the store and participate in the purchase of a replacement.

- Repair—repairing broken items. Children too young to make repairs should be with the one who does the work, so they can develop a sense of appreciation for the effects of their irresponsibility.

- Restoration—cleaning up any mess made—no matter how long it takes. Children too young to do it by themselves should be required to help in some way.

3. They must do a biblical research report on their problem area of sin, and create a plan for their own repentance.

4. Penalties should be increased in proportion to the number of offenses; repeated infractions should be treated as rebellion.

REWARDS VS. CONSEQUENCES

What does a parent do whose child is always distracted and never seems to complete a task in a timely manner? What about a kid that taps his pencil incessantly, constantly annoying everyone around him? What can be done about the preschooler who doesn't seem to work hard at potty training? These types of behaviors are not typically indicative of passive defiance (although it *is* possible they are) and therefore cannot be cured by chastisement. In fact, chastising a child who is *not* in rebellion is a great way to exasperate and demoralize him.

Parents must consider the possibility that the child who fails to compete assignments or doesn't seem to get the hang of potty training, simply lacks the skill to do it. Most children, being young and inexperienced in life, have many skills to learn. It is therefore critical for parents to learn to distinguish the difference between a "will" issue and a "skill" issue.

WILL ISSUES AND SKILL ISSUES

A *will* issue is when a child intentionally resists parental leadership. With their actions or attitude, they say, "I do not accept your authority to make decisions in my life." It is possible that the defiance is simply an expression of a will that has never been subdued. But it is also possible that defiance in an older child is rooted in exasperation or a broken relationship with parents. More on cultivating relationships in chapter 17.

A *skill* issue, simply put, is when a child lacks the physical skill or mental dexterity to do what they were told. They heard, "You have one hour to clean your room," but they lack the mental discipline to stay focused and keep from getting distracted. Threat of chastisement will not typically sharpen their mind, but the right kind of incentive will. This is where rewards come in.

As discussed in the previous chapter, children must never be offered bribes to reduce defiance and gain cooperation.[12] In line with the Scriptures however, it is appropriate to give *rewards* for faithfulness in duties and for learning new skills.[13]

The difference between meriting a bribe and a reward must be understood. A bribe is an incentive to get a child to fulfill a moral obligation—something that he *must* do and has the *ability* to do. A reward is given to reinforce achievement of non-moral goals. If you have a child that never seems able to stay focused on a task, try offering a reward as incentive.

Here are a few ideas for rewards:

- Immediate reinforcement, i.e., a treat for making it to the potty in time; treat breaks for diligent work; money for finding Mom's lost keys, etc.

- Accumulated points for prizes, i.e., toys, tools, outings, etc. Keep track on a wall chart using stickers to symbolize progress.

- Greater privileges, i.e., more gratifying responsibilities like graduating from the push mower to the driving lawnmower, driver's license for faithfulness in duties, etc.

* * *

As we administer discipline to our children, it is critical that they enjoy the security of our love. It is possible for a parent to follow the steps I have outlined and produce highly obedient children.

---

12   Exod. 23:8; Eccles. 7:7b.

13   Matt. 25:21: "His master replied, 'Well done, good and faithful servant! You have been faithful with a few things; I will put you in charge of many things. Come and share your master's happiness!'" Luke 16:10; 19:17; 1 Cor. 3:8; 2 John 1:8.

However, the goal is not merely to control *behavior*—it is to influence their *hearts*. Our children's ability to sense our love is what allows us to influence their hearts. Before you start to implement the disciplinary strategies you have learned so far, I want to encourage you to read the entire book, especially chapter 17, in which I discuss how to connect with your children's hearts.

7

WHAT'S GONE WRONG WHEN CHASTISEMENT DOESN'T WORK?

Many parents cannot subdue their child's will through chastisement, because they are busy strengthening it in other ways.

The first goal of child training is to subdue a child's self-will, and chastisement is God's primary means of accomplishing that goal. Many parents, however, find themselves unable to subdue their children's wills, no matter how faithfully they administer chastisement. Their wills, in fact, seem to grow stronger every day. Such children not only continue in willful disobedience, but they manifest many of the traits of a self-indulgent child, and the home bears the marks of a child-run home. Parents faced with this problem need to consider the possibility that although they practice chastisement as a discipline, they are working against themselves by accidentally fostering self-indulgence and strengthening their children's wills in other ways. The following list offers various subtle ways parents inadvertently strengthen their children's sense of self-importance and send the message that their personal happiness is supreme.

HOW WE ACCIDENTALLY FOSTER NARCISSISM, STRENGTHEN THE WILL, CREATE A CHILD-RUN HOME, AND KEEP OUR CHILDREN IMMATURE

1. We foster narcissism and strengthen the will by removing many of life's obstacles and exempt them from facing unpleasant circumstances. Instead:

- Resist the temptation to always grant children immediate gratification. It is important for them to learn to wait.

- Do not allow them to interrupt conversations. Permitting interruptions reinforces to them that they are the center of the universe and that what they want is of more importance than whatever anyone else is doing or speaking about.

- Do not drop everything and run to *them* when they call you. Rather, require them to come to you, unless it is an emergency.

- Do not jump to provide activity for them when they complain they are "bored." (A good response to the child complaining of boredom is, "I'm glad to hear you are bored. You will find as you grow older that life is full of boring moments, so it is important for you to get used to enduring boredom now.")

- Do not fear canceling plans for fun family events, just because you do not want your children to suffer the disappointment. Make or change plans according to what is wisest for everyone involved. Keep in mind that maturity is developed by learning to work through disappointments.

- If they complain about bread crusts, do not cut them off their sandwiches.

- Do not feed them every time they claim to be hungry. (Children around the world learn to live daily with hunger pangs. Our children can certainly endure them for an hour. Although, most of the time, when a child complains of hunger, he is not hungry at all—he is really just bored.)

- Require them to work daily around the house.

- When your guests have children younger than your children, require yours to get outside themselves, be friendly, and be hospitable hosts.

- Do not allow them sloppy work habits and messy rooms.

- Require them to pay their own bills in life and suffer the consequences for their choices.

2. We foster narcissism and strengthen the will by feeding their appetite for pleasure. Instead:

- Resist the compulsion to provide for them all the pleasures you can afford. They must learn that they cannot have everything they want in life. Children who are never deprived of anything nice grow up intolerant of life's trials.

- Do not deprive them of fun, but do not feel the need to give them all the latest toys, fashionable clothes, etc.

- Immaturity is fostered in children by gratifying all their desires for entertainment and spontaneous fun.

- Avoid giving them multiple opportunities for "escape," such as lots of TV, music, DVDs, comic books, and video games.

- Help them learn to phrase their requests, "May I please?" rather than, "I want."

- Do not make a bag of snacks readily available to your toddler for constant snacking.

- Help them avoid the thinking that life is about leisure and recreation by not enrolling them in every sports and social program they desire.

3. We foster narcissism and strengthen the will by allowing unrestrained self-expression and venting of passions. Instead:

- Do not permit undisciplined communication. Require that they speak with self-restraint, i.e., no whining, grumbling, yelling, swearing, etc.

- Do not allow them to punish the family with their sulking and pouting.

- Permitting them to say anything they feel like saying reinforces to them that the expression of their feelings is more important than the feelings of those they might be speaking to.

- Discourage the "venting" of anger by permitting them to hit a pillow. (Prohibiting them from taking their anger out on something will not make them victims of "repressed" emotions or warp their "psyche." It will teach them godliness. Children must learn that self-control and forgiveness are godly responses to anger.)

- When they are upset, do not allow them to cry uncontrollably for as long as desired.

- When they receive a gift that they don't value, do not permit them to complain about it. Teach them not just to express thankfulness, but to be grateful. Gift giving is not about the *recipient*, but about the *giver expressing love*. Gifts are defined as anything they receive that they did not earn, i.e., birthday and Christmas presents, all meals, clothes, their home, warm bed, etc.

- Do not permit them to vent their destructive tendencies, i.e., don't hide the new magazines from toddlers and give them old ones to tear up. Give them old magazines and teach them to handle them carefully.[1]

---

1   They must learn to respect all property.

- Do not buy them washable crayons and permit them to color on the walls and furniture. You will not "suppress their creativity" by requiring them to color only on paper.

4. We foster narcissism and strengthen the will by allowing them to influence family decisions when young. Instead:

- Children need to understand they aren't in control. They develop humility and self-restraint by learning to cooperate with their parents' leadership. Those children who are granted a say in all decisions affecting the family develop an over-exalted sense of their own importance. This is probably one of the most common ways that parents foster narcissism today.

- Do not have family votes. You may occasionally solicit input from your young children if you want, but be careful of communicating to them that they have a *right* to a say in all family matters. The family is not a democracy, and children can learn selflessness by being required to accept their parents' decisions for them.

- Guard against letting children help decide which restaurant to choose; where to vacation; what type of music the family will listen to in the car; whether or not parents will go out for an evening; what the family will eat for dinner; which church to join, etc. If they ask permission to express their opinion, allow them to, but make the final decision and announce it to them.

- Do not allow them to interrupt parental discussions, and offer their opinions without permission or invitation.

5. We foster narcissism and strengthen the will by allowing them to make too many personal decisions too young. Instead:

- Do not give them many choices. In the first five years of their life do not ask them about their preferences. You decide what they will eat, what they will wear,[2] how they will spend their free time, etc. Neglect of this principle is one of the surest ways to strengthen their wills and increase their narcissism. You can be certain that the majority of narcissistic teenage monsters today were catered to by well-meaning mothers who didn't know that the first five years of life were to be spent cultivating self-control.

- Make decisions about their day. Allowing young children to make "non-moral" decisions throughout their day seems harmless, but granting them that much autonomy over their day sends them the message that they are in charge of themselves.

- Be a strong leader. For proper development a four-year-old needs strong leadership to respond to. If throughout his day, he is allowed to decide what clothes to wear, which toys to play with, what cup to drink from, which room to play in, which book Mom will read him, which side of Mom he will sit on while she reads, etc., don't be surprised if he looks at her at naptime and thinks, "I've been in charge of myself all day—who do you think you are to tell me I have to take a nap now?"

- Give them structure. Children whose days are loosely structured and who make most of their own decisions, typically resist their parents' efforts to assert authority.

---

2   If you like, to prepare them for when they pick out their own clothes at age six, as you select their clothes for church, explain to them the factors involved, such as colors, patterns, and appropriateness of style.

- Plan their time. Parents will notice that during winter and summer vacations, when school-age children have so much unstructured time, they will be more apt to misbehave. Nothing wrong with creating a schedule of chores and activities to offset excessive free time.

- Do not *always* allow them to decide what they will order at restaurants. On occasion, exercise your parental prerogative of ordering for everyone, i.e., "We are all getting the pancake special." (You are giving them a gift and it is appropriate that they only express thanks for it.)

- Do not frequently allow them to do whatever they desire, i.e., while Mom is shopping, Dad follows three-year-old Junior through the mall, permitting him to wander wherever he wants to go, giving him guidance only when in danger. Dad thinks he is developing in his son courage and an explorer spirit, but at age three, he needs to be learning to follow leadership, not exercise it.

6. We foster narcissism and strengthen the will by allowing "substantial compliance."

- When commands are clearly stated, and you settle for less than you requested, you teach them that you do not really expect them to obey, and you strengthen their resolve to pursue their own plans in the future.

- If you tell them to sit down in their high chair, but they squat instead, don't say, "Close enough!" and settle for less than what you requested.

- If you say, "Put this away in your room," and you later find it dropped in their doorway, yet you do nothing about it, you reinforce their self-will.

- If you ask them to come to you, and they make a detour on the way, do not content yourself that they finally arrived. You must bring a consequence.

- If you say, "Eat the rest of it," and they leave half of it, you must bring a consequence. Do not allow your exhaustion or fear of conflict to cause you to accept partial obedience, lest they be strengthened in their resolve to do the same next time.

- If you set a standard for a clean room, hold them to it, or you will find they "substantially comply" the rest of their lives.

- Obedience without humility is not true obedience, but is an expression of rebellion. If they obey, but with complaining and backtalk, their wills remain strong.

- Children who are allowed to compromise parental commands are being allowed to negotiate for a settlement. By no means are their wills subdued.

- If we allow our children to substantially comply with our commands, it may be that we dread conflict and want to avoid it, or we simply do not want to stop and take the time and energy to chastise. Whatever the reason, our children are strengthened in their wills.

7. We foster narcissism and strengthen the will by engaging in and then losing "will marathons." Instead:

- Do not even start a will marathon. Give them a command and bring consequences if they disobey.

- If you say, "You will sit there until . . . " and then cave in, you blatantly strengthen them.

- If they sulk or whine and you finally give them what they want, you subtly strengthen their will and reward their whining, thereby encouraging further whining from a stronger willed child.

- If you hear yourself saying, "I've told you 100 times tonight . . . ! Oh, well, go ahead . . . " you know for certain you have strengthened their will.

8. We foster narcissism and strengthen the will by administering discipline inconsistently.

- If children are to be trained, rules and consequences need to be reinforced consistently. "Hit or miss" discipline encourages children to risk misbehavior, because rules enforced haphazardly are like being given occasional permission. In the words of Rick Fugate, "A child is the only person in the world who will play Russian Roulette with five of six chambers loaded."

- The parents who do not work diligently to be consistent with rules and discipline strengthen their children's wills. Their hope that their parents will forget keeps their wills alive.

- Rules and consequences that are not written down are easily forgotten by child and parent. Write down your rules.

9. We foster narcissism and strengthen the will by allowing selfishness to go unchecked.

- Sharing is like all other biblical injunctions—we must require it of our children.

- If you permit them to not share their possessions with friends or family, they grow in selfishness.

- Allowing them a bad attitude when they do share keeps self-centeredness and selfishness alive.

- Since there are times when possessions have special meaning, parents might make allowance for exceptions, i.e., a new gift has a one-day "closed" period during which the recipient need not share it, but may if they desire.

Perhaps something of sentimental value or something they have been instructed to treat very carefully need not be shared.

A toy need not be shared with another child who has proven irresponsible in the past.

A bike or other "tool" may be exempted, because it has utilitarian value and it is important to minimize the chance of loss or damage.

Because some children have a track record of being rough with possessions, it would be reasonable that no sharing would be necessary with that child.

- Parents best teach selflessness by example.

- Remember the goal is not to force sharing—it is to foster kindness and not permit selfishness.

10. We foster narcissism and strengthen the will by permitting disrespect for others.

- Allowing them to be ruled by their whims, desires, or curiosity, with little or no regard for others' possessions, privacy, or peace, breeds a strong self-interest.

- See chapter 10, "Raising Respectful Children."

11. We foster narcissism and strengthen the will by feeding the ego. Instead:

- Do not reinforce their vanity by placing great importance on how impressively they must dress or groom themselves. Avoid talking a lot about their appearance.

- Guard against emphasizing *competitiveness* over *doing their best*. Giving winning a higher priority than glorifying God puts their eyes back on them.

- Do not overdo praise. Flattering children by constantly telling them how they are the best increases pride—not humility.

- Affirm them with "Pauline praise." In his epistles, the apostle Paul affirmed others' not by flattering them, but by thanking *God* for their godliness.[3] Drawing their attention back to God rather than to them will help maintain their humility.

12. We foster narcissism and strengthen the will by being abusive, both physically and emotionally.

- Attacks against children can create emotional wounds that cause intense self-focus and overwhelming concern for self-preservation, long into their adult life.

- Abused children sometimes behave compliantly, but do so out of a strong commitment to self-protection, not a weak self-will. Their strong self-will may not surface until years later during marriage, when they crave, but fervently resist, physical or emotional intimacy.

13. We foster narcissism and strengthen the will by rewarding defense mechanisms.

- The parents who are fooled by their child's defense mechanisms will fail to cause their child to take responsibility for his actions, and thereby allow his will to remain unsubdued.

- This is discussed further in chapter 9, "How Children Avoid Personal Responsibility."

---

3   Rom. 1:8; 1 Cor. 1:4–5; Phil. 1:3; Col. 1:3–5; 1 Thess. 1:2–3; 2:13; 3:9; 2 Thess. 1:3; 2:13.

14. We foster narcissism and strengthen the will by allowing them nonstop lobbying privileges.

- Children permitted to push and nag their parents are exercising and strengthening their tenacity and determination for getting what they want.

- The time and mental energy given to pursuing what they want increases self-centeredness.

- A child allowed unrestricted lobbying privileges misses great opportunities to grow in self-restraint.

15. We foster narcissism and strengthen the will by justifying all your instructions to your children.

- Wise parents make their children wise by passing on to them the wise reasoning behind parental decisions. However, the parents who feel the need to *justify* and prove the wisdom behind all instructions send the message to their child that they are accountable to him, and that he is owed an explanation.

- Such a child will perceive himself in charge of his parents and will be angered by their chastisement. (See chapter 3, "Why Children Must Learn to Obey without Knowing the Reasons behind Their Parents' Instructions.")

16. We foster narcissism and strengthen the will by ceasing a time of chastisement before it succeeds.

- A child who is not required during chastisement to accept responsibility for what he has done will not be humbled, and will perceive his parent as unfair.

- The parent who tries to bring humility to his child through chastisement, but does not succeed, only frustrates his child and strengthens his will more and more each session.

- See chapter 6, "How to Tell When a Time of Chastisement Is Completed."

17. We foster narcissism and strengthen the will by modeling a strong will.

- Children often learn willfulness by watching their mom's or dad's example. Parents who refuse to submit to authority, whether God's or man's, teach their children that what *they* want is more important than what *others* want or need.

- The primary way children glean values is not from their parents' instruction, but from watching what their parents typically get worked up about.

- Parents who are self-indulgent, angry, or stubborn, should not be surprised to find themselves raising strong-willed children.

18. We foster narcissism and strengthen the will by being sure blessings are kept equal between children.

- Some parents try to keep family peace and minimize life's disappointments by being certain that each of their children receives the same gifts or good experiences enjoyed by their siblings, i.e., when one child receives a gift from someone, the parent goes out and buys the others an equal gift. When one sibling is invited out by a friend, the parent insists that the others go along.

- By keeping all things equal, we teach our children that they are *owed* blessings. Such children will feel deprived, and will tend to mope or wallow in self-pity, when they do not receive equal blessings as others.

- This fosters self-centeredness. Growing in love will require that they learn to rejoice for others.

19. We foster narcissism and strengthen the will by allowing unchecked rebellion.

- Blindness to your child's rebellion allows it to fester and grow.
- See chapter 6, "How to Identify Rebellion."

This chapter lists only nineteen ways parents strengthen their children's wills, but there are many more. Wise parents will comb their parenting practices to discover how they might accidentally be hurting their own efforts to train their children.

8

RAISING RESPONSIBLE CHILDREN

The child who is faithful and reliable in duties is well on his way
to maturity.

I n parenting, one of our goals is to raise children who accept
responsibility for themselves and for their actions. We want
them to be reliable and conscientious in their duties, and to
be honest enough to admit their failures and weaknesses. Those
children who grow up without learning responsibility are not
prepared for adulthood, and will inevitably find themselves
causing grief to all those who rely upon them.

Put simply, there are three basic attributes of responsible
people:

1. They believe it is their duty to provide for themselves.

   • Unless forgiven a debt, they feel it is their obligation
     to pay their own bills.

   • They do not expect others to assume responsibility
     for them.

2. They are faithful and conscientious in duties.

- They have a strong sense of obligation to fulfill their duties and do not stop until job is complete.

- They have personal integrity and can be trusted to do what they say.

- They are self-disciplined—not ruled by laziness or the desire for pleasure.

3. They accept blame for their mistakes and will not shift it to others.

- They accept accountability for their actions.

- They don't make excuses or project guilt to others.

- They do not view themselves as "victims," blaming others for their own poor choices.

- They hold no one else responsible for their reactions; they can handle insults and inconsideration.

- They are honest enough to admit failures and weaknesses.

Although loving parents will want their children to grow in personal responsibility, they may accidentally do much to hinder the process. In the name of "devotion," they protect their children from the consequences of their actions—they effectively *coddle* them. Children raised in this fashion grow up irresponsible and dependent on others to take care of them. When their children grow up, these parents are the ones who ask, "Where did we go wrong? We did everything we could to give them a happy childhood."

Is the answer obvious to you? Parents raise irresponsible or unappreciative children by *doing everything they can to make them happy.* In an attempt to give them a fulfilling childhood, they fail to give them the more significant experience of taking responsibility for themselves.

TIPS FOR TEACHING CHILDREN TO ASSUME RESPONSIBILITY FOR THEMSELVES

Do not do for your children that which they need to do for themselves.

- If they dirty something, they must clean it.

- If they leave a door open, they must go back and close it.

- If they leave something on, they must turn it off.

- If they leave a chore unfinished or poorly done, they must redo it until it is done properly. Do not do it for them no matter how much you fear it will never be done right.

- If they break something, they must pay for it. If they are too young to have money, they must assist their parent in its repair or attend the purchase of a new one. If they are in adolescence, give them a deadline for payment and don't lead them by the hand to find the means of earning the money. If you loan them the money because something must be repaired immediately, do not forget the debt or neglect to collect.

- If they are expected to pay for a new toy themselves, do not back down and make up the difference. Make them save a little longer.

- If they make an unwise business decision, or make a foolish purchase, let them live with their choices.

- If they are of driving age, but irresponsible in life, do not allow them the privilege of a driver's license.

- If they are in trouble at school or their behavior lands them in jail, make them live with the consequences of their actions. Don't bail them out.

- If they use illegal drugs, do not give them clean needles.

- If they are sexually promiscuous, do not give them birth control.

- If your daughter is pregnant, do not help her abort the child.

HOW TO AVOID CODDLING CHILDREN

To coddle children is to cripple them by assuming responsibility for that which belongs just to them. Parents coddle because it comes from the heart and feels so compassionate. Nonetheless, it keeps kids irresponsible, immature, and entitled. Consequently, most coddled children grow up with a victim mentality, viewing life from the perspective, "My problems are some else's fault—someone needs to rescue me."

- Do not wake them daily when they are old enough to set an alarm, or you will create dependence.

- When teens get up late and miss the bus to school, do not be too willing to drive them or write them an excuse if other transportation is available, such as a city bus or their feet. Let them be late.

- Do not give a teen last-minute lunch money or make an extra trip to school if they continually forget their lunch or do not allow time to make it. Let them fast.

- Do not do their homework assignments for them.

- Do not always give them a second chance when they continually fail to comply with standards, i.e.,

    In an effort to get away with little work, their first efforts at cleaning their room are sloppy, but they know that all you will do is point out their mistakes and give them another chance. Why should they try so hard the first time?

    Their first effort at a math assignment is feeble, because they know you will simply point to their mistakes and give them another chance or two.

- Do not state for them, time after time, the established guidelines for chores and standards for behavior.

- Do not give them constant reminders to do their duties. It causes them to grow dependent on you to remember their responsibilities and inhibits the development of independence and self-reliance.

- Parents should be ready to follow through with every consequence or they should not propose them. Do not make empty threats, i.e., "If you're not ready, we're leaving you behind." "If you don't have it done, you're not going." "If you want to buy it, you must pay the entire amount." "If you complain about the food, you'll go without," etc.

The fundamental principle is that a child should be held responsible to do everything he is capable of doing, as young as possible.

DETERMINING IF YOUR CHILDREN HAVE LEARNED RESPONSIBLE WORK HABITS

Signs of Laziness:

- Expects each day to offer fun instead of work; shows great disappointment when wishes for recreation go unfulfilled.

- Avoids work; attempts to persuade parents that there is a better use for their time; offers excuses why they are unable to work; begs to have workload reduced.

- Avoids the task-assignor.

- Does as little as possible; works slowly.

- Puts off starting a job; chooses to play before work.

- Works inefficiently, i.e., with one hand, sitting down, carries one at a time, etc.

- Does an incomplete job; quits before finished; jobs performed sloppily with little attention to detail.

- Negotiates with a sibling or friend to do the job.

- Constantly looks for breaks; leaves the job early.

- Finds multiple excuses to stop work, i.e., bathroom breaks, drinks, looking for tools, etc.

- Intentionally works slowly or does such an inadequate job that the parent takes over and finishes the task.

- Sleeps-in every opportunity; stays in bed after called.

- Works for "eye service"; only works hard when being supervised.

- Constant, unrelenting daydreaming.

- Disappears when he thinks job is completed and neglects to ask if there is anything else to do.

- Chooses sedentary recreational activities. (Not necessarily a sign of laziness, but can be a sign when considered with other signs.)

DEVELOPING RESPONSIBILITY AND GOOD WORK HABITS

As most people make the transition from adolescence to adulthood, they discover that adulthood brings with it tremendous responsibilities. Many are unprepared for the demands of adult life, and never seem to "get the hang of it," so they fail miserably in careers, finances, and relationships. They were not prepared by their parents, so lack the maturity to successfully handle life. Do you want your children to grow up without maturity like so many who struggle today?

In almost every culture in the world before the twentieth

century, parents trained their children to assume adult responsibilities in their teen years. Since the beginning of human history, people married and entered careers as teens. Parents understood that growing in maturity required children to learn while young, that life is about *responsibility*—not idle gratification and pleasure. Parents knew that the sooner children learned to be responsible, the sooner they matured. We need to implement that same principle with our children.

This idea is a foreign concept to many modern parents who have grown up in affluent America. They believe that since children have only one childhood, it should be the most exciting and entertaining it can be. To them, childhood is not a preparation time for adulthood, but is a time of ease and freedom from responsibility. Instead of teaching children to do as much as they can as early as they can, they encourage them in self-gratification well into their twenties. These parents misunderstand parental nurturing, and coddle their children long after they are capable of caring for themselves and serving others. To them the very suggestion that children should preoccupy themselves with learning to be *responsible* and not with *play* is offensive. If that is you, please reconsider.

PRACTICAL WAYS TO CULTIVATE A HARD-WORK ETHIC:

1. Schedule weekly and daily chores.

2. Give them responsibilities congruent to their age capabilities.

   - Reject the idea that childhood is a time to be *free* from responsibility. It is the time for *cultivation* of responsibility. The goal is to bring them to maturity so that by the time they are teenagers, they will more than succeed in whatever they do. The belief that childhood is all about play and fun has produced a generation of immature teens and adults.

- The fundamental principle: A child should be held responsible to do everything he is capable of doing, as young as possible, i.e., a fifteen-month-old can begin to learn to pick up his toys; a seven-year-old can learn to do his own laundry.

3. Reject the notion that it is a mother's job to do all the work in a home. It is the duty of both parents to train the children to be responsible.

4. Tolerate no bad attitudes about work. If they regularly complain, it is likely that they are not yet used to work as a normal part of life. They have developed a worldview around their own pleasure, so view work as an intrusion to their fun. Their bad attitudes will improve once their worldview adjusts to reality.

- Cure their perspective by scheduling more regular chores.

- If they already work without complaint most of the time, but are starting to express discontent or lazier work habits, consider the possibility that you are actually overworking them and need to give them more breaks.

5. Motivate the development of work skills by offering simple rewards for work well done. After all, the Bible says we will be rewarded for our faithfulness in duties.[1]

- Rewards can be interspersed throughout the day, i.e., on a hot summer's day, as an incentive, you can have them look forward to a swim or some other refreshing activity after a couple hours of labor.

---

1   1 Cor. 3:8: " . . . each will be rewarded according to his own labor."

- Rewards can be granted at the culmination of a project, i.e., they can look forward to a day trip at the culmination of a weeded yard.

6. Increased work privileges can be a tremendous incentive for good work habits. Jesus did teach that he who is faithful in little is entrusted with much.[2]

- Tell your lawn-mowing children that if they prove responsible and diligent with the push lawnmower, they will one day be entrusted with the driving mower.

- If your children are faithful as meal preparation assistants, graduate them to meal preparers.

7. Teach them a motto and occasionally have them repeat it while working, i.e., "Work hard, work fast, don't stop, look for more."

8. For irresponsible or lazy *older* children, postpone their meals until they complete their tasks.[3]

9. Do not pay them for fulfilling their duty to their family.[4] Do not pay them to babysit their own siblings—family looks after family. They wash the dishes because they help dirty them; they vacuum the carpet because they play on it; they carry the firewood because they are warmed by it, etc. If you want to give them spending money, do so because they are faithful members

---

2   Matt. 25:21: "His master replied, 'Well done, good and faithful servant! You have been faithful with a few things; I will put you in charge of many things. Come and share your master's happiness!'" Luke 16:10; 19:17.

3   2 Thess. 3:10: "For even when we were with you, we used to give you this order: if anyone will not work, neither let him eat."

4   Luke 17:7–10.

of the family, but not because they need to receive monetary recompense. If you want to pay them for work around the house, let it be for a job you would typically hire out.

THE RESULTS OF HARD WORK

Most parents find that children who grumble and whine when they are first learning to work, eventually discover great satisfaction in a job well done. Children raised to work hard as a normal part of life are typically at an advantage over others in school and in the workplace.

1. Our joy is full when we actively love and serve others.

> If you keep My commandments, you will abide in My love; just as I have kept My Father's commandments, and abide in His love. These things I have spoken to you, that My joy may be in you, and that your joy may be made full. This is My commandment, that you love one another, just as I have loved you. (John 15:10–12)

2. We grow to maturity when we endure "suffering." The challenge of hard work certainly qualifies as "suffering" (Heb. 2:10; 5:8–9).

3. Youthful diligence bears lasting fruit.

> The sluggard craves and gets nothing, but the desires of the diligent are fully satisfied. (Prov. 13:4)

> Lazy hands make a man poor, but diligent hands bring wealth. (Prov. 10:4)

If we are overindulgent parents, having as our highest goal to give our children fun, fulfilling childhoods, our children will learn to equate joy with *fun*. They must learn, however, that the greatest joy comes not through abundant recreation, but through a job well-done, and more specifically, through serving others.[5] If you desire for your children a fulfilling childhood and a satisfying life, then teach them responsibility by teaching them to love[6] and serve others.[7] (Further discussion in chapter 17.)

RAISING CHILDREN TO BE ACCOUNTABLE FOR THEMSELVES

It is in human nature to avoid pain, be it physical, emotional, or social. Since Adam first blamed Eve for his decision to eat the forbidden fruit,[8] people have been shifting responsibility for the mistakes they make and the wrongs they do. It seems that nobody wants to get into trouble. Consequently, it is our children's nature to blame someone or something else for that which is their responsibility. Yet, maturity requires that an individual hold himself accountable for that which is his fault.

Unfortunately, in modern America, the tendency to hold others responsible for our mistakes has become epidemic. Children grow up and blame their parents for their "issues." Incarcerated criminals blame the cops or their victims for their jail sentences. The adulterer blames his coldhearted wife for his philandering. The majority of people, it seems, see themselves as "victims" and therefore not completely to blame for their failings. If our children are to become emotionally mature, they must learn from us to take responsibility for what they do. The worst

5   John 15:10–12.

6   John 13:34; 15:12; 1 John 3:23; 2:8–11; 4:21; 2 John 1:5–6; 1 Cor. 9:21; Rom. 13:8–10; James 2:8.

7   Gal. 5:13–14; John 13:14–15; Gal. 6:2, 1 John 3:16; Eph. 5:2; Rom. 12:10.

8   Gen. 3:12: "Then the man said, 'The woman whom You gave to be with me, she gave me of the tree, and I ate.'"

thing for them would be to grow up with a "victim mentality" that would relieve them of responsibility for their choices and their responses to life.

In addressing "victimization," Solomon put it this way: "He who conceals his sins does not prosper, but whoever confesses and renounces them finds mercy."[9] In other words, those who disavow responsibility for their actions or reactions reap emotional or spiritual bankruptcy, while those who admit their failings enjoy mercy.

IDENTIFYING A "VICTIM MENTALITY"[10]

If we want our children to grow up mature and not as "victims" who justify themselves and blame others for their actions and reactions, we must distinguish between true and false victims, or better yet—*full* victims and *semi* victims.

A *full* victim is a passive recipient of harm. It is one who contributed nothing to his affliction and lacked any capacity to control its effects. Full victims are completely *innocent*. In this category are adults who have suffered child abuse, domestic violence, rape, or other kinds of criminal assault. It includes those who are genetically predisposed to a disease, victims of drunk drivers, and children who contracted AIDS in utero. Few will dispute that these people and others like them are true victims and deserve our utmost care and mercy.

Semi victims are those who may suffer a mishap or incur a condition, but are not innocent—they have contributed in some way to their affliction, even if it is just in their reaction. Included

---

9   Prov. 28:13.

10   Parts of the following section were adapted from chapter 8 of my book, *Born Liberal, Raised Right.*

in this category are smokers with lung cancer, athletes injured in sports, and prostitutes with STDs. It also includes incarcerated criminals, sexually active teenage mothers, and street people, not to mention lazy students who earn low grades, sugar-eaters with cavities, and bullies who lose fights. They still deserve our compassion and care, but in some way they are victims of their own choices and are reaping what they have sown.

It is the *semi* victim who most often develops a "victim" mentality. This mentality is illustrated by the following three perspectives:

- "Someone else is responsible for the problems I have brought upon myself."
- "Someone else is responsible to rescue me from my hardships."
- "Others are responsible for how I respond to them."

"Someone else is responsible for the problems I have brought upon myself."

People with a victim mentality overlook the fact that they contributed to their condition. In their minds, someone or something else is liable for what they have done. They have lots of excuses, and their explanations and justifications lift the burden of guilt. This shifting of responsibility means they may blame the innocent for problems they have brought upon themselves. And if the "victim" has been *forced* to reap the consequences of their foolishness or misdeeds, they will blame the one who reports them or executes justice. Examples:

- Billy is in trouble for stealing cookies intended for the family's dessert, but he holds his sister responsible because she told her parents he was the thief.

- Sarah is startled by her baby brother's sudden cries, so she is angry with him when she drops her ice cream cone.

- Johnny has been caught writing bad things in his sister's diary, but says it is her fault since she left it out in plain sight and didn't lock it up.

"Someone else is responsible to rescue me from my hardships."

Victims think they shouldn't have to live with the consequences of their actions. And because they hold others responsible for the afflictions they bring upon themselves, they think it is someone else's duty to rescue them. In their minds, they are entitled. At the least, they believe their condition, or the afflictions they have suffered, earns them special treatment. I have observed that even full victims can be so deluded by self-pity that they develop the perspective that "everybody owes me." Examples:

- Bobby wastes his money on candy instead of saving it for the trip to the amusement park, and then gets angry with his parents when they won't give him spending money the day of the trip.

- Despite warnings from her parents, Sally left her bike out in the driveway overnight and it was stolen. Now she expects them to buy her another one.

- Junior is only seven years old so when he breaks a window, he anticipates his parents will replace it and he won't have to use his birthday money.

- When Junior breaks his playmate's toy, he expects that his parents will pay for a new one. When he is sixteen, he assumes they will pay for his parking tickets. When full grown he will demand that the government provide free condoms and abortions since his parents have taught him that he shouldn't have to live with the consequences of his bad choices.

"Others are responsible for how I respond to them."

The concept of "victimization" is based on the idea that I am not in control of myself—that who I am and how I respond is determined by someone or something else. I am at the mercy of people and things that influence me. I will, therefore, hold them responsible for the reaction evoked in me.

This element of "victim" thinking is deeply rooted in all of us, and might manifest throughout our day. Consider the "victim" elements of the following phrases:

- "See what you made me do?!"
- "Can't you see what you're doing to me?"
- "I wouldn't have done what I did if you hadn't done what you did to me!"

Yes, those phrases might be uttered by innocent victims who had no choice in their response. But more often than not, we and our children speak them when we want to blame someone else for our *reaction*. The truth is we cannot blame others because we do not respond well to what they do. Each of us is accountable for our responses.

If our children are to reach maturity, they must learn from us that when they endure a negative action, they are still accountable for their *reaction*. We must hold them responsible for that which is under their control. That is what Jesus meant when He taught, "Love your enemies, do good to those who hate you, bless those who curse you, pray for those who mistreat you. If someone strikes you on one cheek, turn to him the other also. If someone takes your cloak, do not stop him from taking your tunic. Give to everyone who asks you, and if anyone takes what belongs to you, do not demand it back."[11]

Unfortunately, we may be unable to teach our children that they are responsible for their responses because we have not learned it yet ourselves. We may justify ourselves and hold resentment against those who offend us. When we reap bad results from our own mistakes or choices, we may blame someone who isn't responsible. Solomon notes, "A man's own folly ruins his life, yet his heart rages against the LORD."[12] Yes, we may even blame God when we have contributed to our own troubles. To help our children reach maturity, we must accept that we are responsible for the outcome of our choices and decisions. We must stop exempting ourselves from godly reactions no matter what the degree of offense we feel.

HELPING CHILDREN TO OWN THEIR RESPONSIBILITY IN LIFE

1. Model personal responsibility and not defensiveness.[13] If you do not model this, all your teaching and correction will amount to just empty words. Do your children hear you blame others for your poor responses to them? Do they see you place fault somewhere other than yourself when you make a mistake?

2. Study the next chapter and identify your children's defense mechanisms. Start holding them responsible for their behavior. As you read through the next chapter, ask God to reveal your own methods of avoiding personal responsibility. God must open our eyes, because we tend to be blind to our faults and

---

11   Luke 6:27–30.

12   Prov. 19:3.

13   John 13:15; 1 Cor. 4:16; 11:1; Phil. 3:17; 2 Thess. 3:7; 1 Tim. 4:12; Titus 2:7; Heb. 6:12; 13:7; 1 Pet. 2:21; 5:3.

bad habits. As Solomon says, "All a man's ways seem innocent to him, but motives are weighed by the LORD."[14]

This issue of blindness to personal responsibility is especially evident in the area of mental health. A key trait of many who are mentally unstable is that they have an inadequate view of personal responsibility. They typically blame others for their condition, and only begin the path to recovery when they start to accept responsibility for their responses to life.

3. Do not rescue your children from every playmate who offends them by scolding the offender or intervening to make everything fair. Instead, help them view their offenders through the eyes of love. A child who is continually rescued from offensive people grows up without social resilience and a tendency to see themselves as victims deserving of pity or special protection. The political correctness plaguing modern civilizations is rooted in a lack of social resilience fostered throughout childhood. Too many people grow up these days unable to endure others' bad opinions of them.[15]

4. To help children learn to own their responsibility in life, we must require that they properly make amends for harm they cause others. This means making reparations to whoever was harmed by their misdeeds. Reparations include cleaning, repairing, or replacing whatever was lost or damaged.[16]

When our children are making amends for the harm they have done, keep in mind that a proper apology does not remind the offended person of how he provoked the problem, i.e., "I'm sorry I hit you when you were being such an idiot to me." The reality is our children must learn that it is never okay to be an "idiot" and it is not okay to respond to an "idiot" with violence. Self-restraint is the mark of maturity.

---

14   Prov. 16:2.

15   Prov. 12:16: "A fool shows his annoyance at once, but a prudent [mature] man overlooks an insult."

16   Prov. 14:9a: "Fools mock at making amends for sin . . . ."

5. A time of chastisement is when our children's sense of personal responsibility is greatly tested. In the face of imminent consequences, they will be tempted to disavow or minimize their part in a misdeed. During such a time, it will therefore be necessary that parents take heed to the following:

    a. Require your children to acknowledge what they did to deserve disciplinary consequences. Emphasize to them that their choice is what merited them consequences. What they have done is no one else's fault. You might even quiz them before chastising, "I know your brother did a bad thing to you, but did that make it okay to paint his hamster blue?" or "Is there ever a good reason to steal your family's dessert and eat it? What consequences must come to those who make such a choice?"

    b. Permit no excuses or justification of wrong behavior. Don't encourage them to make excuses by asking them "Why did you do such a thing?" Is there ever a good reason to do evil?

    c. Forbid implication of others. Do not allow them to blame anyone else for their *reactions*. Remind them that it is never anyone else's fault when we choose to do wrong. Assure them that you will deal with the others separately.

    d. Chastise them when they try to make you feel guilty for your handling of the matter. Our children must learn from us that guilt projection is intolerable.

Children who are taught to take full responsibility for themselves, their actions, and reactions are well on the way to maturity.

9

HOW CHILDREN AVOID PERSONAL RESPONSIBILITY

The ten-year-old child who accepts personal responsibility has greater maturity in many ways than the fifty-year-old adult who blames others.

One of the key ingredients to maturity is the ability to take responsibility for oneself and one's actions. Our discipline of our children, therefore, becomes useless, and even harmful, if we carry it out, but fail to cause them to accept responsibility for their misbehavior. In order to help our children take responsibility for themselves, we must be aware of the methods and tactics which can be used to fool us. The following list is the result of years of cataloging the methods of avoidance used by most people—children and adults alike. As you study through the list evaluating your children's behavior, don't be fooled by your own defense mechanisms and miss the application in your own life.

HOW DO CHILDREN AVOID TAKING PERSONAL RESPONSIBILITY FOR BEHAVIOR?

1. Denial—a willful refusal to even *consider* their contribution to a problem; a dangerous form of *self-deceit* that fosters lying. Denial says, "It's never my fault." Some level of denial is at the root of most defense mechanisms.

2. Rationalization—avoiding taking full responsibility for behavior by means of excuse and self-justification. Those with this propensity to rationalize their behavior often deceive themselves with extensive reasoning, and feel misunderstood.

3. Partial Confession—acknowledging that something bad has happened, but stating it in a way which ignores or avoids their responsibility, i.e., "The lamp broke," rather than, "I broke the lamp." It is very important in confronting our children that we teach them to assume responsibility for themselves by making clear confessions of their mistakes or sins.

4. Discreditation—ignoring their parent's confrontation by discrediting them in their own minds through faultfinding, i.e., "You criticize me for that? Well, who are you to talk!? You do the same thing." Often this is learned by watching their parents do it with each other.

5. Guilt Projection—disavowing personal responsibility by casting the blame onto someone or something else. Adam first did it—blaming God for giving him Eve.[1] Children who hold others responsible for their own mistakes and failures may develop the "everyone owes me" mentality, i.e., "I'm never responsible for anything wrong in my life. It's always someone else's fault." Those who feel the world is in debt to them may employ some method of *"emotional manipulation"*

---

1   Gen. 3:12.

to make others feel guilty or responsible for their difficult situation. They may even have the audacity to become angry with those who fail to take responsibility for them, and are rarely satisfied with undeserved help they receive. They are often unappreciative for favors given them.

6. Guilt Sharing—accepting blame, but implicating as many others as possible in the crime. The more others are made to look guilty, the less spotlight on the one caught—he is just one of many. Those who confess for others also may hope to be held less responsible, or be dealt with more leniently, because they have been so cooperative.

7. Avoidance—staying away from their parents or others who may confront them about their behavior, i.e., may come home late from school, find excuses to stay at a friend's house, begs to change churches, etc.

8. Minimizing—acknowledging personal responsibility, but downplaying the significance or seriousness of the crime, i.e., "Yes, but what I did really wasn't that bad."

9. Emotional Manipulation—a child's attempt to control a parent by manipulating their most vulnerable emotions and insecurities.

   a. Withdrawal—By retreating into himself or giving off the "silent treatment," a child will attempt to punish and manipulate his parents with guilt. Sulking and pouting are plain attempts to control his parents and influence their exercise of discipline.

   b. Charm—Those children who learn that they are "cute" can resort to playing up their "cuteness" to soften their parents' anger. This cuteness includes well-timed expressions of affection. Many an unwary parent has helped their child learn to escape responsibility by falling victim to charm.

c. Whining—Many children learn to manipulate a parent by wearing them down emotionally with constant whining. Parents finally succumb to the will of the child, giving in to the whining as they would to torture.

d. Emotional outbursts—By an intense outburst of crying, a child can manipulate a parent in two ways:

1.) Tears can evoke compassion and guilt in the parent and halt further confrontation. Attention then becomes focused on the *"hurt"* and *"distressed"* condition of the crying child. A parent can even be manipulated into an apology when this technique is used properly.

2.) Tears can fool the conviction-resisting child themselves. They become so preoccupied with their "distress" that they will no longer focus on their responsibility. For many, this form of self-*pity* is a standard defense mechanism which, if not broken by parents, solidifies in the child an inability to hear correction or reproof as adults.

e. Departure—In an attempt to play on their parents' insecurities, they will suddenly storm out of a conversation or run to their room. They are playing the games, "If you really love me, you will follow," or possibly, "You've really done it now—I'm hurt!" Again, if successful, they can evoke an apology. (A parent should also consider that despite the disrespectful departure, their child may have been genuinely hurt.)

f. Intimidation—A child who subconsciously perceives himself as in control of his home will be furious that his parents have had the audacity to thwart his will. By throwing a tantrum, blowing up into a rage, or by maintaining an irritable mood, a child can unnerve an insecure parent. Fearing the loss of their child's approval, they may compromise the exercise of their authority, inadvertently preserving their child's control of their home. A child's anger may also intimidate those who simply dislike conflict or those who mistakenly think they have pushed their child to the point of exasperation.

g. Patronization—Because some children hate tension or conflict, they become agreeable to everything said by their parent. Although they do not believe what they are agreeing to, they are accommodating to appease their parent, thereby diffusing the tension, and bringing to a close the time of confrontation. A child doing this may often leave angry, and feeling unjustly accused.

h. False Humility—In the midst of confrontation, a child might acknowledge his guilt, but overstate it with the intent of evoking compassion and mercy in his parents. His self-depreciation may even cause his parents to minimize the sin, saying something like, "Don't be so hard on yourself. You're not that bad."

i. Penance—They do something good to make up for doing something wrong, so they will not have to humble themselves to ask forgiveness, i.e., they pick you flowers, draw you a picture, cuddle with you, etc. Keep in mind that these manipulative acts of "affection" are done in *place* of taking responsibility for a wrongdoing, and are not to be confused with genuine acts of affection that might accompany confession and repentance.

10. Redirection—directing a conversation away from himself by changing the subject. The following are typical means of *redirection* a child might use to take the attention off of himself:

a. Accusation—He will find fault with his parent. If he can get his parents on the defensive by pointing out their failures, he will take the heat off himself and focus the attention on them. It may also be an effective means of guilt projection and emotional manipulation.

b. Flattery—He will stroke his parents with the intent of getting them more concerned about themselves than him. This buttering up of their ego may also cause them to lighten their discipline on him, since he has now made them feel good about themselves.

c. Embarrassment—By making a scene in a public place, many children successfully change the focus of a conversation. This is commonly done with an emotional outburst involving anger, crying, or a raised voice.

d. Division—"Divide and conquer" is the concept behind this one. If a child can play one parent against the other, he can divert their attention to a power struggle between them, thereby potentially weakening the discipline he faces.

e. Diversion—A simple diversion to a completely unrelated subject; accomplished by either asking an unrelated question or by bringing up a new subject. This includes intentionally misinterpreting something which has been said and going into great detail addressing an unrelated topic.

f. False Confession—When the parents are probing too closely to the root cause of their adolescent child's personal problem, he may make a false confession. By acknowledging an unrelated or more socially acceptable sin than the one he knows he is actually guilty of, he keeps his parents off track, and can continue in his ways. His confession may even impress them as *humility*.

11. Exemption—Many children discover early in their lives that a debilitation or "handicap" exempts them from complete responsibility for their actions. Not many children are aware that feeling sorry for oneself fuels self-exemption, because the very nature of self-pity is to blind. They may even learn to welcome debilitations or to create problems for themselves that cause others to become more tolerant and understanding of their misbehavior.

> ***a. Sickness***—Some children find such solace in the tolerance shown them during an illness that they convince themselves they are sick much of the time. If their parents or others do not sufficiently exempt them from their responsibilities, then they wallow in self-pity, believing that they are being unfairly treated. If this pattern of self-exemption is not stopped while they are young, by the time they reach adulthood, they will be victim to one psychosomatic disorder after another.

> ***b. Fatigue, Hunger, and Irritability***—Many parents excuse their children's misbehavior if the hour is late or if they have missed a nap. This reinforces to the child that they needn't always exercise self-control. Those who have heard their parents announce the "reason" for their misbehavior may even learn to feign sleepiness or hunger as an excuse. Parents may be amazed to discover that a fussy child can exercise self-control if required.

> ***c. Physical Injury***—We properly respond with compassion and expect less "action" from children beset by an injury. Many children however, learn to make the most of injuries, no matter how minor, to gain exemption from their responsibilities in life. This ploy is especially effective for a child seeking to escape accountability for his part in a conflict with another child. Parents, take note—when you pick up your little one to confront him on misbehavior, does he suddenly assume a pitiful expression on his face, point to an old scab or scar on his leg, and say, "I hurt myself"?

d. Emotional Injury—In the same way that those with physical injuries exempt themselves from physical activities, those who perceive themselves as victims of "emotional injuries" may exempt themselves from their roles and responsibilities, both spiritual and social. As real as the pain is from emotional wounds, Jesus tells us that we are not to maintain anger or bitterness against those who hurt us. Bitterness and unforgiveness may never be excused with the phrase, "I'm just hurt." Anticipating his people would not be exempted from the physical and emotional abuse in this world, Christ commanded that we love, bless, and pray for those who hurt us. We are always called to love and forgive as Christ loved and forgave His persecutors. We must teach our children that they are not exempted. (One tip: before speaking to the child about the need to forgive, be sure to express compassion for them first.)[2]

e. Rejection—One of the most difficult sights for a parent to see is his child crying because of rejection of his peers. Parental comfort is a powerful and appropriate balm to that child's ailing heart. However, some children are very self-centered and have a difficult time developing relationships. Parents must be careful to not exempt their self-centered children from learning the selflessness required of friendships. That child who is allowed to wallow in rejection and self-pity, and is not trained to take responsibility for himself, will always lack social maturity, and may eventually develop a subtle type of persecution complex.

f. Shyness—Though some children are more introverted than others, many learn to use their "shyness" as an excuse to be exempted from uncomfortable social situations, i.e., they offer silence in response to an adult's

---

2   Rom. 12:15.

greeting or hide behind your leg; they are old enough to make a phone call, but insist that you call a store for them when they have a question; they refuse to apologize for a wrong they have done to another. A child may have a quiet personality, but shyness is no excuse for poor manners and subsequent hurt feelings. A refusal to be polite is a matter of will. Children as well as adults, when faced with any unpleasant task, must put aside their own personal comfort and do what is loving toward others.[3]

g. *Labels*—Many children are born with or develop physical disabilities or chemical imbalances which affect the control they have over themselves. These handicaps may include learning disabilities, Attention Deficit Disorder (hyperactivity), autism, etc. As real and disabling as these conditions are, some children learn to use their "label" to their advantage. They hear their parents excuse their misbehavior to others, so they misbehave knowing that their "condition" exempts them from the standards of behavior expected of others. When they have been disobedient or unruly, they may tell others things like, "Well, I'm A.D.D. you know," or "I'm a little wild today, because I didn't have my pill this morning."

12. **Selective Hearing**—hearing or remembering only what they want to hear. Although a discussion, confrontation, or words of advice may be clearly spoken, some children may glean only the words or phrases that are *useful* to them. They may twist phrases or take words out of context to later justify misbehavior, conveniently blaming their parent for their actions. Listening selectively means that after a recon-

---

3   Phil. 2:3.

ciliation session with his sister, Johnny may recall only that which applies to him. He may "mishear" and then misstate what was said because he wants an excuse to disregard the confrontation. He may even misconstrue the truth as an excuse for his reaction of self-pity or emotional outbursts, i.e., sulking, tears, rage, etc.

13. Blocking—a firm, resistant denial of what is being said, related to selective hearing. The child in this case refuses to hear or consider anything contrary to their beliefs or practices. Either their mind is made up or their heart is so hardened that they cannot even begin to consider what is offered them. Those who "block" respond to confrontation as if they didn't hear it. They tune it out. Too much is at stake for them. Acknowledging the validity of what is said will require them to change, and they do not want to. Subconsciously, they may agree with their parent, but they will not admit it, lest they feel guilt.

14. *Self-pity***—feeling sorry for oneself excuses one from personal responsibility by concentrating attention on one's "oppressed" and "victimized" condition. Those children using self-pity consume themselves with the hurt from "unfair" treatment they have received. Not uncommonly, they are bitter and unforgiving toward those they hold responsible. One using self-pity as a defense mechanism feels "picked on" and is prone to sulking, pouting, and whining to solicit pity. Frequently, they will tell their "story" to anyone who will listen, just to garner sympathy or support for their side. Self-pity can be a strong factor in denial, guilt projection, rationalization, emotional manipulation, redirection, selective hearing, and exemption. Ultimately, the self-pitying child rarely solicits pity by appealing directly to others, but their manner seems to say, "Aren't I pitiful? I am so unresponsible for what has happened to me. I am such a victim of others—don't you just feel sorry for me?" Parents duped by self-pity will withhold needed correction because they feel sorry for their child.

A WORD OF CAUTION

The parents who are freshly aware of their children's methods for escaping responsibility may be tempted to become suspicious of everything their children do. Every tear, every hurt, and every appeal for sympathy may possibly now be regarded with mistrust. Such automatic mistrust is not good.

Parents, you must be careful of allowing your new knowledge to overshadow your natural compassion. Watch yourself. Do you hear yourself thinking things like, "You're not going to fool me, kid. I'm onto your game." If so, then you are out of balance, and you may begin to exasperate your child.

Remember, Jesus told us to be as "wise as serpents, and as harmless as doves,"[4] but He also told us that love "hopes all things."[5] Do not be fooled by your children, but do not automatically think the worst of their motives either. Don't forget that you use defense mechanisms too and God is merciful to you. He is not postponing His acceptance of you until you finally get your act together.

If you discern your child is using one of these methods of avoiding personal responsibility, the goal is not for you to simply recognize it, but to train your child to be aware of it and turn away from it. You want them to learn to become honest with themselves and others.

---

4   Matt. 10:16.

5   1 Cor. 13:7.

10

RAISING RESPECTFUL CHILDREN

Children, obey your parents in the Lord, for this is right. "Honor your father and mother"—which is the first commandment with a promise, "that it may go well with you and that you may enjoy long life on the earth."

—Ephesians 6:1–3

WHY IS IT IMPORTANT FOR CHILDREN TO LEARN TO RESPECT ADULT AUTHORITY?

The Bible commands not only that children respect their parents, but also like adults, they must give honor to whomever honor is due.[1] They are to behave respectfully toward all those in authority, whether it is a schoolteacher, a babysitter, a governing official,[2] a police officer,[3] a church leader,[4] or just someone older.[5] It is important that children learn to respect all adult authority for several reasons:

---

1   Rom. 13:7; 1 Pet. 2:17.

2   1 Pet. 2:13–14.

3   Rom. 13:1–5.

4   Heb. 13:17.

5   Lev. 19:32; 1 Tim. 5:1; Job 12:12.

- Learning to honor adult authority when young prepares a child for future adult responsibilities in areas of work, social relationships, and citizenship.

- Being required to behave and communicate respectfully teaches a child self-restraint and reinforces to them that not everything they feel or think need be expressed.

- Learning to honor adult authority when young prepares a child to respect God's authority.

WHAT IS RESPECT?

Hebrew

kabad, kaw-bad'; literally—to be weighty, i.e., to take seriously; to regard with sobriety.

yare', yaw-ray'; to fear; to be frightened of; i.e., to revere or treat with reverence.

Greek

timao, tim-ah'-o; to esteem and place great value upon; to revere; to show honor.

phobos, fob'-os; to regard with fear or fright.

WHAT DOES IT MEAN TO SHOW RESPECT FOR AUTHORITY?

Based on the Greek and Hebrew word meanings, there are two elements of *respect*:

1. To treat those in authority with the realization that they have power in your life. It means that when they speak, you listen and obey them, fearing the consequences they could bring for disrespect.

2. To behave in a way which shows value to the one deserving of honor. Most significantly, respect is more a *behavior* than it is a *feeling.*

Conversely, *disrespect* is showing disregard or contempt for authority; communicating little regard for the office or station in life of another. It is treating parents or any adult with the familiarity appropriate a peer.

EXAMPLES OF DISRESPECT TOWARD ADULTS

Defiant Attitude

1. Knowingly disobeying direct commands or ignoring wishes; i.e., active or passive rebellion.

2. Threatening statements such as, "I can't wait until I'm old enough to move out of here!"

3. Rude, intentionally hurtful remarks such as, "I hate you."

4. Grumbling about any parental decision qualifies as disrespect. Objections such as, "That's a dumb idea," are insulting. Threats such as, "I'm going to have a rotten time," are not only impolite and ungrateful, but attempt to manipulate a parent.

5. Speaking in an irreverent manner such as with sarcasm or a voice raised in anger.

6. Storming out of the house, slamming doors, etc.

7. Defiant statements such as, "I'll do it when I get around to it," or responses such as, "Yeah, yeah, yeah." "Hold your shirt on." "Whatever!" "Don't have a cow."

8. Trying to show they are unfazed by discipline; accepting it casually with an attitude of "no big deal."

Inappropriate Familiarity

1. Scripture indicates that children are not the social equals of adults, and therefore should not be allowed to treat them as peers. We are to treat others with honor in respect for their age and station in life, i.e.,

> Rise in the presence of the aged, show respect for the elderly and revere your God. I am the LORD (Lev. 19:32).[6]

> Do not rebuke an older man harshly, but exhort him as if he were your father. Treat younger men as brothers, older women as mothers, and younger women as sisters, with absolute purity (1 Tim. 5:1–2).

> Show proper respect to everyone: Love the brotherhood of believers, fear God, honor the king (1 Pet. 2:17).

As indicated by the following passages that describe degenerating societies, one sign of a family in trouble is disrespect for parents and the elderly:

> The people will be oppressed, everyone by another and everyone by a neighbor; the youth will be insolent to the elder, and the base to the honorable (Isa. 3:5 NRSV).

> Princes have been hung up by their hands; elders are shown no respect (Lam. 5:12).
> Brother will betray brother to death, and a father his child. Children will rebel against their parents and have them put to death (Mark 13:12).

---

6   God regards respect for the elderly as part of our worship of Him. See also Prov. 16:31; 20:29; Job 32:4–6.

2. Allowing children to call adults by their first name grants them peer-level status, and shows no honor for their station in life.

Physicians are addressed as "Doctor" by their patients, but are on a first-name basis with their peers. In the military, higher-ranking officers are addressed as "Sir" by those under their command, but are on a first-name basis with their fellow officers. Many schools have found that those teachers who allow students to address them on a first-name basis, may be popular with the students, but are often less respected by them.

Children are not the peers of adults, and therefore should be required to address them with respectful titles, i.e., Mr. and Mrs., Aunt and Uncle, Sir, Ma'am, etc.7

3. Calling parents derogatory names is disrespectful, no matter how innocent sounding, or how playful the context, i.e., "Dad, you dummy!"

4. Taunting or teasing communicates disrespect. If teasing is unacceptable toward children, it is even less appropriate toward parents, i.e., when you ask for them to pass the butter, they hold it out to you, but just out of your reach.

5. Giving orders, even playful ones, such as, "Say, 'please'" is inappropriate and unacceptable.

6. Children who yell for parents to come to them, rather than going to the parents, show no regard for the importance of what their parents might be doing. In recognizing the Father's greater position, Jesus once said, " . . . I am going to the Father,

---

7   Keep in mind that the goal is to show honor, so if an adult insists that a child call him by his first name, it would be dishonoring to insist that your child still address him with a title.

for the Father is greater than I."8 It is appropriate for children to call for their parents to come to them in emergency situations, but not to look at a plaything they constructed.

7. Snide looks, rolling of the eyes, mockery, or teasing of adults; comments like: "Ha, ha, so funny I forgot to laugh," might be tolerable banter with peers, but are too familiar with those worthy of respect. Dad's jokes may be corny, but he may not be mocked for them.

8. Unless it is an emergency, children should never be permitted to criticize those over them in authority, make fun of their failures, or correct them without first securing their permission, i.e., if you are telling your spouse about an incident that happened last week, when your child interrupts your conversation to declare that the incident happened not last week, but two weeks ago, they are correcting you and should reap a disciplinary consequence. What constitutes an "emergency" might be when your child overhears you giving someone inaccurate directions. At that point, it would be appropriate for them to politely interrupt, "Dad, may I interrupt? Isn't it left on Elm Street, not right?"

9. Children should not be permitted to "bad mouth" any adults, even those whose behavior may be severely wrong, or those you may deem worthy of disrespect, i.e., an absentee father, a hostile neighbor, an anti-family politician, etc.

Concern for Self Over Others

1. Ungratefulness shown for a gift given them shows contempt and disrespect for the feelings of the giver. Children must learn that the feelings of the giver are more important than the satisfaction of the recipient.

---

8   John 14:28; 13:16.

2. Complaining about what has been given them for dinner or what has been ordered for them at a restaurant is impolite and ungrateful.

3. Silence in response to an adult's greeting is impolite. Shyness is no excuse for bad manners and hurt feelings. A refusal to be polite is a matter of will. (Even though it is not comfortable for them to meet someone new, they must not be permitted to refuse to be polite, and greet them.)

4. Interrupting adult conversations when not an emergency shows they think that what is on their mind is more important than what others are doing or are talking about. They must be trained to consider the impact of all their actions on others.

5. Disturbing others in public shows a preoccupation with personal pleasure and a lack of consideration for others' privacy or peace, i.e., playing in a store, excessive noise, running in a mall, playing a portable stereo loudly at the beach, etc.

6. Taking the best seat and releasing it to an adult or a guest only under coercion shows a concern for personal comfort over others.

Giving Sass or Backtalk

1. Simply put, sass is any response to an adult statement that is given without *permission* or *invitation*:

- Denying responsibility;

- Questioning or challenging;

- Offering unsolicited explanations during correction; or

- Grumbling or blurting out objections about parental decisions.

2. Contradicting a parent's statement is the same as calling them a liar. If a child believes his parent is mistaken about something, then he should be allowed to offer his opinion, but only after he has secured his parents' permission to do so.

3. If you allow them to continue to sass throughout childhood, they will make themselves obnoxious to their future employers and will limit their success in social relationships as well. Sass is a form of defiance and reveals a lack of submission to authority.

4. Sass is any response except, "Yes, Dad," "Yes, Mom," "May I appeal?" or some other respectful request for permission for further discussion.

RESPECTFUL RESPONSES TO PARENTAL INSTRUCTIONS

It is important that children learn to respond to all parental instructions or requests with a verbal affirmation that they heard and intend to carry out the instructions. A child who is allowed to remain silent in response to instructions has not agreed to anything and may not fulfill parental expectations. Respectful responses are ones that indicate humble subjection to authority, such as:

- "Yes, Dad"

- "Sure, Mom"

Children should be able to make appeals for discussion, but only if they show respectful subjection to authority, and first secure permission before offering their questions or thoughts. Possible appeals:

- "May I appeal?"

- "May I have your permission to discuss this?"

- "Excuse me, Dad, may I offer you new information before you decide?"

- "May I inquire as to your reasoning?"
- Or occasionally with teens, "Excuse me, Dad, may I have a chance to talk you out of this?"

Whatever the appeal process we give our children, they should never be permitted to respond with "sass" or "back talk." If they respond argumentatively, or with anything other than a pre-established respectful response, then we must guard ourselves from responding to them with anything except correction. To answer them or continue in dialogue is to reward them and encourage future sass. Those children who abuse the appeal privilege by appealing every instruction should have it revoked for a time.

TEACHING RESPECT FOR OTHERS AND THEIR BELONGINGS BY REQUIRING CHILDREN TO ASK PERMISSION

In the military, a soldier shows his respect by requesting permission to speak before offering his ideas or asking questions. In business, a wise worker asks permission of his boss before taking a vacation. In court, attorneys do not tell the presiding judge what to do, but humbly make requests. Asking permission is an important demonstration of respect for others and acknowledgment of their authority. A child who does not ask permission, but presumes to proceed with his own plans, is exercising authority he has not been granted. He is demonstrating a "respect" for his own interests over the interests of another. It is imperative that children learn to show respect for others by asking permission. The following are typical situations in which asking permission would be appropriate:

- They touch or pick up something which belongs to another, i.e., toys at the home of a friend; mail on the kitchen table; a freshly glued piece of china drying on the counter; a mouse trap behind the dryer; the refrigerator handle, Dad's tools, etc.

Respectful approach: "May I play with this toy?"
"May I touch this?" "May I eat this?"

- In response to instructions, they ask "Why?" without first securing your permission.

    Respectful approach: "May I have your permission to ask why?" "May I appeal?"

- After receiving instructions or correction, they walk away from you before being formally dismissed.

    Respectful approach: "Is there anything else? May I go now?"

- Going off to play after deciding they have completed enough of their chores.

    Respectful approach: "Mom, I've finished my chores, is there anything else you need me to do, or may I go off to play now?"

- They overhear a parental conversation and offer their opinion when they have not been invited.

    Respectful approach: "May I offer my vote on where we go out to dinner tonight?" "Would you be open to hearing where the kids would like to vacation this year?"

- *Telling* you rather than *asking* you things, i.e., "I'm going next door to play"; "I'm going to spend the night at so-and-so's house this Friday"; "I'm going to get a cookie"; "I'm not going back to that school!"

Respectful approach: "May I go next door to play?"
"May I have something to eat?"

- Responding to instructions with statements rather than with questions, i.e., "I'm not going to bed that early"; "I'll be there in a minute—I'm getting a drink first"; "But I don't want to . . . !"

Respectful approach: "May I stay up later?" "May I get a drink first?" "May I offer you my ideas?"

The general rule for our children: If you have not been granted authority, do not make decisions on your own. If it does not belong to you, do not touch it. If you have not secured permission, do not offer your opinion.

11

EXPECTATIONS FOR DIFFERENT CHILDREN AND DIFFERENT AGES

Sometimes, a child is not as handicapped by his condition as parents are by their low expectations.

One of the biggest obstacles in successful parenting is ignorance of the capabilities of a child at each stage of development. Typically, first-time parents are most aware of their ignorance and ask questions like, "How old will she be before she can sleep through the night?" or "When can I expect my little one to obey me?" Sadly, the ones often giving them advice are old-time parents who themselves lack proper understanding about children's capabilities. Unaware that children need not go through modern phases like the "terrible twos" and the "trying threes," they infect first-time parents with the misconceptions they developed from their own experiences with improper training. And the cycle continues.

When looking at various cultures throughout the world, one realizes that God has equipped children with far more capabilities than most American parents understand. In many socially undeveloped countries, children can work capably and diligently at home by five years of age. In those same "backward" countries, young men might be starting their careers by age twelve. One need only look back in American history to discover the same thing.

In 1778, John Quincy Adams served in an ambassadorial post in the court of Catherine the Great in Russia—he was fourteen years old. In 1813, U.S. naval officer David Farragut commanded a captured British vessel—he was twelve years old, having begun his naval career at nine. These men were not unique in their culture. They were typical of the young adult teens of their day. Needless to say, preschool-age children were beyond our modern youngsters in areas of personal responsibility. What we must learn from this is that unruly two-year-olds and rebellious teenagers are creations of our modern approach to child rearing.

Does the thought of an eighteen-month-old sitting peacefully during Sunday morning worship service appeal to you? Can you imagine a den in which the stereo does not have to be moved out of reach from a toddler because he has been trained to not touch? Are you able to envision a home where the Christmas tree is not kept safe in a playpen and where eight-year-olds do their own laundry? Children are far more capable than most parents realize.

In order to bring our children into their greatest potential, we must lose our fear of warping their little "psyche" by requiring submission of their will to ours. We must not be afraid of "robbing them of their childhood" when we emphasize responsibility before play. Let us be careful of selling our children short when we say things like, "Kids will be kids," or "They're only children." Yes, they are not as capable as adults, but they are far more capable than we give them credit.

WHAT CAN BE EXPECTED AT WHAT AGE?

Susanna Wesley wrote as one of her rules in her "Plan of Education":

> "When turned a year old (and some before), they were taught to fear the rod and to cry softly, by which means they escaped abundance of correction which they might otherwise have had . . ."[1]

Mrs. Wesley had found that children were capable of understanding correction by one year of age. Her conviction was not unique. Parents throughout history have held a similar philosophy. How far we have fallen!

The premise for training children is the same no matter what their age: If they can understand you, they can be trained to obey you.

HOW CAN PARENTS TELL IF THEIR CHILD UNDERSTANDS?

Consider the following exercises:

- *Tone* and *manner*: By nine months old, children may not understand all your words, but most can read your *tone* and *manner*. They understand a firm No perfectly—that is why they cry in response.

- *Restraint*: The crawler who struggles to get down from your arms should not be rewarded. Be sure to say No and hold him tight until he stops struggling, and then do not put him down for a while. He is smart enough to learn that when Mommy or Daddy initiates an action, he is to submit to it.

---

1   Cited by Rebecca Lamar Harmon, *Susanna, Mother of the Wesleys* (Nashville, TN: Abingdon, 1968), pp. 58–59.

- *Offering a treat*: To test a toddler's understanding of your vocabulary, without showing him anything, offer him a familiar treat, like ice cream or a bottle. Does he respond? If he does, then he is old enough to understand a simple direction such as, "Come here, son," and should be chastised each time that he chooses to defy your authority.

- *The clap*: If your crawler reaches for the stereo, walk over, offer a firm No and clap your hands once. If they respond to your voice and the sharp sound of the clap and turn away, they got the message and should be held accountable from then on. You may even want to skip the clap.

BUT MY CHILD IS DIFFERENT!

Yes, your child is different. All children are different from one another, just like they will be when they are adults. One is proficient at math and another is better at spelling. People are born with different personalities and therefore, different capabilities. Some are more proficient in the areas of art, athletics, humor, intelligence, and social awareness. Some can sit for hours and read, while others always lose at Freeze Tag, not realizing that their "frozen" body is in constant motion.

Some children learn and progress at faster paces than others. Some cannot seem to remember anything and others remember too much. Yes, children are all different, but God's standards are the same.

CAN DIFFERENT CHILDREN BE HELD TO THE SAME STANDARD?

It is true—every child is different from all others, but that does not mean they can be held to different standards. God's standards are the same for everyone. Kindness is kindness, respect is respect, obedience is obedience, and rudeness is rudeness. God's standards do not change from child to child—they may be harder to achieve with one child than another, but like God, His standards are eternal and unchangeable.

DANGERS OF THE STATEMENT "MY CHILD IS DIFFERENT"

The statement, "My child is different," is a dangerous statement. In one context, a parent may say it simply referring to the personality differences between children, but all too often it is an attempt to justify a child's disobedience or disrespect. Sadly, parents who dismiss their child's rudeness, spite, or selfishness as just a personality bent or response to hardships, ultimately handicap themselves in their parenting. Parents must know their children are capable or they will not hold them to God's standard.

Often, the parent who believes his child is just "different" is really saying, "I've tried my best and I don't know what else to do." The good news is that there is hope. Your child may simply have become a victim of your blind spots. It could very well be that this book will be the avenue of transformation in your home.

WHAT ABOUT SPECIAL NEEDS CHILDREN?

Special needs kids are just that—*special*. They may be handicapped by autism, retardation, or brain damage. Possibly they have been diagnosed with Attention Deficit Disorder,[2] or they may have been a drug baby who still suffers the side effects of their birth mother's heroin addiction. For their parents who know and love them, these children can be a source of joy, but as those same parents may testify, they can also be a source of great grief.

---

2   Although the validity of ADD as a scientifically provable "disability" is understandably questioned by some, its predictable patterns of behavior, at the least, are indicative of inherited personality traits.

For with the delight of parenting comes the pain of watching your child struggle with anti-social behavior, which brings them rejection from others and trouble at home.

Some parents of special needs children find consolation in knowing that their child's misbehavior is rooted in a chemical imbalance or a brain dysfunction, but that comfort may vacillate, depending on how much stress they cause at home. Many of these parents, distressed by their child's misbehavior, are haunted by the nagging question, "Is there something else I can do?" There certainly is.

With such varying degrees of mental handicap facing different children, a common basis for determining trainability must be established. The parent of each child must determine, "To what degree has my child shown himself to be trainable in the past?"

Parents have to determine: can they . . .

- feed themselves?

- dress themselves?

- visit the toilet by themselves?

- get a drink of water from the tap?

- operate a DVD player?

- complain when they are unhappy?

If they can do these things, how did they learn—by direct training and by watching? If they have shown they are trainable, why stop there?

Yes, they may have a brain dysfunction or chemical imbalance, but that is no excuse for rebellious, disrespectful, or unruly behavior. When you walk together, do not pull them by the arm or drag them along—require them to walk obediently with you. At meal times, unless they lack motor coordination, do not permit them to eat like a pig. When they are greeted by family friends, do not permit them to scream or run away. In being introduced to someone new, require them to be polite and to speak respectfully.

Yes, they are harder to train than a "normal" child, but God's standards are the same. In fact, the parent must apply the same principle of child training to the special needs child as to any child:[3]

- Work to subdue the will.

- Bring it into complete subjection to yours as early in their life as possible.

- Don't compromise God's standards. (Just as shyness is no excuse for rudeness, ADD is no excuse for a lack of self-control.)

- Whatever moral behavior you want, set that as your goal, and go for it.

- That goal will be more difficult and may take longer to achieve than with a normal child, but it absolutely must be done. The longer one waits, the stronger the will grows, making it more difficult to subdue as the years go by.

PARENTS, HAVE HOPE!

Sometimes, a child is not as handicapped by his condition as parents are by their low expectations. The parents who expect little of their child inadvertently degrade him by accepting that

---

3   Even many levels of autistic behavior, if caught early enough, can be trained out of a child. Such a child is not easily brought out of his self-involved world, but many parents who have given themselves to the time-consuming training testify to its effectiveness.

soul-less animals are more trainable. Consider that since, contrary to their nature, wild animals can be domesticated and trained to perform difficult feats, we can be sure that special needs children can be trained as well! Few parents would admit they believed that their children were lower in ability than animals, but their low expectations of them infer it.

MY PERSONAL NOTE TO THE SPECIAL NEEDS PARENT

Of my six children, two were clinically diagnosed with Attention Deficit Disorder. Over the years, we went the route of medications and support groups, but nothing affected our children's behavior like the principles of biblically based child training. Some research suggests that dietary treatment for conditions like ADD and autism may be helpful, but balancing the body chemistry is no substitute for proper training. As parents of "special needs" children, we must be careful of allowing rebellious or disrespectful behavior, because we imagine it impossible to train our children to behave otherwise. Let us hold to God's standard and persevere in our training.

A key tip I offer any parent, but especially the parent of a particularly challenging child—be careful of allowing frustration to sour you toward him. Listen to yourself—do you place an exclamation mark at the end of that one child's name in comparison to the others? Have you decided that his incessant moving of his body or tapping of his fingers is "rebellion"? Be careful! What we perceive as justified anger will effectively communicate a lack of acceptance. Eventually, that child will not seek acceptance from you, but will find it from someone you will deem a dangerous influence. Be firm, but draw your child into obedience by love and acceptance. Intimidation will not work! (More in chapter 17.)

ONE LAST THOUGHT

I have heard from several different parents over the years who have testified of diligence in training, but saw little fruit with one of their children in particular. Each described their child as highly intense and unable to learn the basics of self-control. None of these children was malicious, but each was driven by impulse and had to be corrected constantly.

Finally, one mother of seven children called to say she had found a solution that transformed her son within weeks. Her "intense" son had suddenly started responding to his training just like his "normal" six brothers and sisters. I listened to her solution, then contacted the other parents I had been trying to help and shared her solution with them. They each tried her solution and then called back a few weeks later to report that they had the same amazing results. Years later, I am still in touch with one of the families and the changes have continued.

The solution that these parents claimed to work for them was in the area of allergies to food additives. They each eliminated certain foods from their problem child's diet and found almost immediate behavior change.

I am a specialist in biblical counseling, so do not feel professionally qualified to evaluate the effect of food additives on the body. However, going on the testimonies of these parents, as well as the testimonies of many more that I since have read, I conclude that desperate parents have nothing to lose by looking into eating plans like the Feingold Diet.[4]

If you are a parent who implements all the principles of biblical child training in your home and one of your children does not respond, it might be worth looking into a diet as an aid. It could be something that makes all the difference.

---

4   In the last ten years, I have become a proponent of natural and organic foods, because my body went through a dramatic healing when I eliminated manmade chemicals from my diet. Ten years ago, the doctor told me that my liver was bad and I would need a transplant within the decade. I didn't want a transplant, so I figured I had nothing to lose by trying a vegan diet of fruits and vegetables for one year. They were organically grown and void of all manmade chemicals. At the end of the year, my body had rebuilt my liver perfectly. I told a friend of my experience because he had a bad liver and was given six months to live. He tried the same diet and six months later, he was healthier than ever and his tests revealed a perfect liver. Neither his nor my experience is adequate scientific proof of anything. However, these experiences have caused me to wonder about the effects of manmade chemicals on the human body. It would not surprise me if food additives affect not only our health, but our brains as well.

12

REHEARSING RIGHT BEHAVIOR

The best defense is a good offense.
—Atilla the Hun

TEACHING OBEDIENCE THROUGH REHEARSING PROPER BEHAVIOR

An important principle of successful repentance, although plainly displayed in the Bible, is often missed by many believers in their reading. Ephesians 4:28 reveals it clearly. There we read, "He who has been stealing *must steal no longer, but must work,* doing something useful with his own hands, that he may have something to share with those in need" (emphasis is mine). We are told here, as we are throughout the epistles, that we are not simply to cease from *wrong* behavior, but instead are to do *right* behavior. Trying to stop sinful habits without replacing them with righteous ones will frustrate any adult Christian, let alone a child. Anyone who goes out each day and tries simply to "not sin" is bound for failure, i.e., trying to "not be angry" at your boss all day will never get the success as "pursuing love" for your boss.

Our children, in order to learn how to obey us, must understand not only what they must *not* do, but what they are *to* do. This will require us to help them plan proper responses to life and temptations. Not only must we help them identify and plan a path of repentance, but we must prepare them to walk it by rehearsing with them in advance of the situation.

- The parents who know their children tend to give in to their shyness when meeting new adults, can practice in advance of an upcoming encounter. They can role-play the situation and give them the opportunity to rehearse proper responses, i.e., "Hello, Mrs. Smith. Come in and have a seat. I'll tell my mother you're here."

- In a store, when your children start enjoying the displays as a playground, call them over to you and say, "Please come stand by me and be bored." (Remember the best response to the child complaining of boredom: "I'm glad to hear you are bored. You will find as you grow that life is full of boring moments, so it is important for you to learn to endure boredom now.")

- Rather than waiting until Sunday morning and using a church worship service to teach a child to sit still, it is helpful to have them practice at home—not as punishment, but as a training exercise to help them get their little bodies under control. Pull up a chair, and have them sit quietly for increasing increments of time. Try five minutes the first day, ten the second, fifteen the third, and so on. Chastise them each time they get down without permission. Start when they are toddlers and you will be amazed at what they are capable of. This is a very simple means of helping them learn to endure challenges, and it teaches them to accept your authority to make decisions in their life.

- Plan their responses for them, giving them not only the bad behavior to avoid, but the good behavior to pursue:

Wrong: "Johnny, when that boy pushes you, don't fight."

Right: "Johnny, when that boy pushes you, come tell me." Children need their paths clearly laid out for them. Just as they need to know what *not* to do, they need to know what *to* do.

- If you have picked them up and they do not want to be held, do not put them down when they fuss or try to wriggle from your arms. Teach them to ask politely, "May I get down, please?"

- A child who is learning to submit his will to his parents should be required to respond with a *verbal* affirmation to all instructions. It is an important exercise of coming under parental authority and increases the likelihood of obedience. Give them the acceptable responses and have them rehearse saying it, i.e.,

"Yes, Mom" or "Yes, Dad."

"I will obey you, Dad."

"I will stay in bed, Dad."

Children can respond with anything you require of them, like my wife's favorite: "Yes, Mother, most beautiful among women."

Even toddlers with limited speech can learn to be polite, by hearing their parent suggest for them proper polite responses, i.e., after a diaper change, you say for them, "Thank you for changing my diaper, Dad," or after a meal you say, "Thank you for making dinner, Mom."

PICK THE BATTLEFIELD

Rather than waiting until you are pressed for time to train your children, consider setting times for training their wills. Don't wait for them to misbehave, forcing you to act only in response. Instead, plan and initiate time for their training.

For example, if you want your toddlers to learn to obey your word, take ten minutes aside each day to train them to obey your voice. Pick a time in which you will have nothing better to do than train them. Then find them in the house and call them to come to you. Speak to them calmly, and only one time. If they do not come, walk over, pick them up, look them in the eye, and say, "When Mommy or Daddy speaks to you, you must obey," and then administer proper chastisement. Place them down on the floor where they were, walk away from them, and call them again. Repeat the process until they come each time. Walk to different places in the room, or walk out of the room and call them. After they consistently obey, keep practicing with them for a few more minutes. Be sure to praise and affirm them each time they obey, and you will discover that they find joy in pleasing you.

What this accomplishes:

- Typically, within minutes, your children will be capable of obeying you.

- Their wills becomes subdued and they begin the process of learning to say "no" to themselves.

- They become conditioned to respond to your voice.

- As they become conditioned to obey your voice, you will find that their obedience carries over to other areas of life, i.e., they obey you more readily at bedtime, at mealtime, in public, etc.

You can practice with various other basic commands, such as, "Don't touch." "Put that down." "Stop." "Sit down." "Don't move, stay there." "Be quiet—close your lips." The more regularly you take time aside to train your children's wills, the sooner you will see them become ready to receive values instruction.

13

CHILDREN AND FOOD

Starving children in third-world countries are rarely found to be picky eaters.

SHOULD CHILDREN BE REQUIRED TO EAT AND ACCEPT THANKFULLY FOODS THEY DO NOT ENJOY?
(Concerning a Pattern of Pickiness and Not Random Occasions of Appetite Loss)

Reasons Why Parents Are Reluctant to Require Children to Regularly Eat Foods They Don't Enjoy:

- They are concerned children may gag or vomit.

- They fear it will make children have a negative attitude toward food.

- They want to reduce stress at mealtime. It is easier to train their will all day in other areas of home life.

- They are empathetic. They do not enjoy certain foods so do not want to force a child to eat something they do not like.

Reasons Why Parents Should Require Children to Eat Food Prepared for Them:

- Maturity can only be attained by enduring challenges. Requiring them to develop a taste for food they do not at first enjoy teaches them that by self-denial, difficult things in life can be faced and overcome.

- Requiring them to receive the food their parents have chosen for them teaches them to submit to parental authority. In doing so, their will is subdued. If neglected, their will is strengthened.

- Submission to parental decisions teaches trust in parental wisdom.

- Food is an area in which the will is most visible in a young child, thereby providing the *optimum* opportunity to subdue it.

- Moms will lean toward preparing only foods that the children will eat, thereby granting the children authority to control the family menu.

- Food is a gift for which we give thanks—first to God and then to the one who prepared it. We teach our children hypocrisy if we encourage them to thank God for the food He provided and then allow them to continually reject it. (Ps. 145:15; Job 36:31)

It teaches them good manners. Ungratefulness is rude. It is impolite and insulting to refuse a gift, especially one that has been labored over. It is particularly disrespectful and thankless to refuse the food God has provided for the family. Food God provides should be received with thankfulness. (Matt. 14:19; 15:36; 26:26; Luke. 24:30; John 6:23; Acts 27:35; Rom. 14:6; 1 Tim. 4:3–4)

- It will help prevent them from becoming picky eaters. Picky eating is generally considered a negative trait. As adults, they will lose respect when they refuse to eat the food set before them while guests in others' homes.

- Picky eating is a trait found predominantly in a spoiled and affluent society. Starving children in third-world countries are rarely found to be picky eaters. Parents pamper by permitting pickiness.

- If children are consistently allowed to refuse nutritious foods, they will become malnourished.

- Acquiring a taste for food is more easily learned when young. Waiting until adulthood to develop that discipline is far more difficult.[1]

Each child is born with a self-centered worldview and expects his wants to be satisfied. Catering to his flavor and texture preferences only strengthens his narcissism. Parents need to stop asking their young children what they want to eat and start announcing what will be served. If Mom or Dad hears grumbling about the gift (meal) Mom is about to give them, then the children must be instructed that the only appropriate response to a gift is "Thank you." Parents should beware if they hear themselves justifying their decision to cater to the children's preferences with statements like, "My little ones just won't eat such and such." They can eat whatever you decide they must eat.

Requiring our children to eat whatever is given them helps subdue their natural demand for gratification, and they learn that what they want in life is not as important as what their parents want for them. This submission to parents is a key part in the subduing of the self-will and the development of maturity.

---

1   Since taste buds replace themselves every twenty-one days, it only takes that long to develop a taste for new foods.

14

BEDTIME BLISS

Young children don't have problems with learning first-time
obedience—only parents do.

For some parents, the most difficult part of their parenting
day is bedtime. Each night, just when they are hoping that a
quiet household is minutes away, they find children offering
their greatest challenge. If the parent can manage to get them
in bed, they do not lie there, smile and say, "Thank you, and
goodnight." They make multiple excuses to stay awake. Some
beg to stay up, others cry for Mommy to lay down with them or
read them one more story, many get out of bed time after time.
For those parents who find bedtime to be one of the most challenging parts of the day, I offer the following tips:

PREPARATION FOR BED

- **Try to give bedtime warnings**. Do not walk up to your children and suddenly announce, "Bedtime!" without taking into consideration that they may be deeply involved with something. Although children need to be able to respond immediately to sudden parental decisions, keep in mind that it is difficult for most of us to stop in the middle of an intense activity and change course. A five-minute warning each night can make going to bed far less stressful for the child and for you.

- **Allow for a wind-down time.** After dinner, or in the final half-hour before bedtime, permit only quiet activities, which will help their bodies slow down.

- **No caffeine prior to bed.** Many parents sabotage their own efforts to get their children to sleep by serving desserts full of chemical stimulants right before bedtime.

- **Create a bedtime "theme song"** and sing it each night to your toddlers or preschoolers. Start a few minutes before bed, while you change their diapers, dress them, or hold them in your arms. If done consistently, upon hearing the song each night, they will know what awaits them and will be conditioned to accept the inevitable.

- **Be certain that all pre-bedtime necessities have been done** before going to bed, i.e., potty, drinks, teeth brushed, Daddy hugged, rooms cleaned, clothes laid out for tomorrow, etc.

ONCE IN BED

- **No excuses allowed** for getting back up. Establish a rule that once in bed, no drinks may be requested, etc.

- **Spend quality time** with them. Most children will accept any excuse to stay awake, so capitalize on their openness. Take bedtime each night to talk with them about serious things. Talk with them about the Lord—pray with them. Get to know them—ask them questions about their values and dreams. Tell them stories about your childhood. Parents who rush their children into bed each night miss one of the greatest opportunities of building influence with their kids.

- **Establish in your mind that you have nothing better to do** than train your children to stay in bed and you will find yourself less frustrated with them, when they get out time after time.

- **Late naps or no fatigue are not excuses** for a lack of self-restraint. Children can learn to lie still in bed simply because their parents have told them to, whether they are tired or not. Staying in bed is a matter of obedience to parental instructions—not tiredness.

- **When they get out of bed**, do not fret and fume. Say, "Thank you, Lord, that my child's willfulness is so obvious," and then calmly administer chastisement.

- **If bedtime rebellion** persists, and children habitually get out of bed, the cause might stem from one of several factors:

    1. They are willful, because first-time obedience was not required all day. Parents who require first-time obedience during the day have a much easier time at bedtime.

    2. They were granted liberty to make their own decisions all day, so refuse their parents' attempts to exercise authority over them at the end of the day, i.e., they decided which toys to play with, which rooms to play in, which clothes to wear, which books to read, which videos to watch, which plate to eat from, etc. The child who is in charge of himself most of the day will usually challenge his parents at bedtime.

3. They have been having bad dreams and fear going to bed. Parents who allow their children to watch cartoons or movies with aliens, monsters, or demons, should not be surprised that their children's imaginations spawn horrible dreams and nightmares.

4. When extreme fear or panic is the chief reason a child resists staying in bed, consider several alternatives:

- On occasion, lie down with them for a short time.

- Leave the door open and the hall light on.

- Reassure them of the falseness of monsters and that God is bigger than the boogeyman.

- If the fear of staying in bed is not a pattern, invite them to sleep on the floor in your room for one special night. (Emphasize to them that it will be only for one night, so they have understanding when you refuse them the next.)

SUGGESTED SCENARIO FOR TEACHING A TODDLER TO MAKE THE TRANSITION FROM THE CRIB TO THE BED

1. Place them in their new "big bed" and affirm to them how big they are to have it now.

2. After you read to them, talk with them, and pray with them, explain to them that they must stay in bed.

3. Make clear that they must obey Mommy and Daddy and will be chastised if they disobey.

4. Ask them what they heard you say, including what consequences they will face if they get out of bed.

5. Give them the right words: "I will stay in bed, Daddy."

6. Be warm and loving, letting them see tenderness in your manner.

7. Leave the room and wait outside the room with a spanking implement in your back pocket.

8. When they step out of the room, greet them with a serious expression, take them in your arms, and administer a swat of chastisement.

9. It is important to be admonishing them for disobeying you as you administer chastisement.

10. No need for anger. This is when you thank God for giving you a child whose defiance is so easily seen and dealt with.

11. Place them back in bed and repeat the process from point three on.

TRAIN THEM TO PUT THEMSELVES TO BED

Some parents have no struggles at bedtime. In fact, sending kids to bed is not even a part of their daily routine. This is because when the children are old enough to read a clock, they are trained to put themselves to bed when it is time. Yes, this is possible. And why shouldn't it be? If your children recognize your authority and respond with affection to your love, there is no reason why they won't be able to. You may not choose to attempt this, but you certainly may if you desire.

15

EXASPERATING YOUR CHILDREN

Most parents are afraid of exasperating their children by being too firm, but most children are exasperated by parents who are not firm consistently.

25 SURE WAYS TO EXASPERATE YOUR CHILDREN

1. **Never admit you are wrong.** Always insist you are right. Acknowledge no mistakes—excuse, justify, and rationalize every error.

2. **Model hypocrisy.** Hold them to a higher standard than you hold for yourself. Require perfectly of them that which you fail in *miserably*.

3. **Fail to keep promises.** Frustrate them and teach them to mistrust your word by rarely following through on that which you say you will do for them.

4. **Demand too much of them.** Tolerate nothing less than perfection. Catch their every failure and stay on them when they fall short of your perfect standard. Know no mercy.

5. **Overprotect them.** No matter how old they are, limit their freedom and independence. Give them few opportunities to fail. Make all decisions for them, without consideration for their feelings or desires.

6. **Batter them with words.** Rather than responding to misbehavior with appropriate disciplinary actions, habitually lecture them for long periods of time.

7. **Abuse them verbally.** Bark out your orders. Yell at them when they blow it. Let your tone consistently demonstrate harshness. Demean them by name-calling, character assassination, and predictions of failure. Swear at them when they tick you off.

8. **Make discipline too severe.** Mete out consequences that are overly harsh for the crime.

9. **Show favoritism toward their brothers or sisters.** Give unequal disciplines for similar violations. Consistently trust one child over the other. During correction, compare them to their siblings. Respond harshly to one child and sweetly to another for the same infraction.

10. **Embarrass them.** Show them disrespect by scolding or disciplining them in front of others, particularly in front of their teenage friends. Talk openly about their weaknesses and mistakes to others.

11. **Give no time warnings.** When they are in the middle of a fun activity, never give advance warning that it is time to end it. Regularly wait until the last minute and demand them to immediately stop whatever they are doing. (However, because life doesn't always give advance warnings, do not be afraid, when necessary, to teach them to respond to disappointments by requiring that they end their activities abruptly, and with a good attitude.)

12. **Try to be their buddy.** Strive to be their parent and their pal. Tease, chat, and play with them like a peer one moment and step into your superior role to exercise adult authority the next. Permit them to show disrespect to you, teasing you, correcting

you, playfully calling you names, and then turn around and exercise firm authority over them in some matter. Allowing them such over-familiarity will frustrate them, because they will be made to feel like equals *and* subordinates. The insecure parent who needs his children's approval will find his children despising him. Children innately need their parents to be *leaders* not *followers*.

13. **Withhold firm discipline and proper training.** The lack of clear boundaries will make them insecure in your love. The responsibility they will bear in overseeing and making decisions for your family will produce in them anxiety too great for their emotional maturity.

14. **Discipline inconsistently.** Most parents are afraid of exasperating their children by being too firm, but most children are frustrated by parents who are not firm consistently. Enforcing rules inconsistently sets unclear boundaries, which beg to be violated. It is also like giving them occasional permission to disobey. The temptation to risk violating your standards leaves them insecure and anxious. If you make a rule, enforce it. Otherwise, your kids will "stress out" trying to figure when to take you seriously.

15. **Assert parental authority weakly.** Not only will you exasperate your kids with inconsistent discipline, but you will also frustrate them by sending mixed messages. With your lips you will say, "No, and that's final," but you will permit them to bring up the subject over and over, and you may eventually cave in. Your words draw a line, but you allow them to step over it. The parents whose limits are not firm allow their children to partially shoulder responsibility for running the home—a job for which they have not been equipped. They are always planning, plotting, and scheming. There is no rest for the child who is always testing their parents to see how far they can be pushed.

16. **Consistently believe evil of them.** In correcting misdeeds, jump on them like you expected the worst, as if you are

picking up where you left off last time. Communicate to them your mistrust by rarely greeting them with a smile. Let them see you looking at them suspiciously whenever they come into your presence. In correction, remind them of all the times they have failed throughout their lifetime. Give them no genuine fresh starts.

17. **Do not listen to them.** Give them no opportunity for expression of their opinions, complaints, or frustrations. Refuse to allow them to speak their mind, even when communicated respectfully.

18. **Continually criticize and critique them when they share their innermost feelings and thoughts.** When they are being vulnerable, expose their hidden heart motives. Tease them about sensitive issues.

19. **Communicate to them how unwanted they are.** Let them know they are an inconvenient nuisance, that you could have had a successful career if it was not for them. Allow them to overhear you promise others that you will not have any more children, and that you will be glad when they move out of the house. Let them hear you speak to others about "children" with regret or contempt in your voice. When you are angry at them, tell them you hate them.

20. **Threaten them with rejection.** When they misbehave, frequently warn them that they may have to leave home. If they are a child of divorce, hold over their heads that they may have to go live with their other parent.

21. **Never communicate to them approval.** Force them to hunt for it outside the home from their friends, teachers, or youth leaders. Find fault with everything they do. Never allow them to think they have satisfied you.

22. **Neglect them.** Always be too busy to give them *positive* time. Give them attention only when they need discipline.

23. **Overindulge them.** Allow them such an influential voice in family decisions that they will come to expect that they

should have their way. They will think of the family as a democracy, and therefore will resent any parental decisions made without their input. Permit them so many personal decisions when young, that by their teen years, they will think they have a right to run their own life. Grant them so many of their wishes, that they will think they are owed everything, and will appreciate nothing.

24. **Reward insolence.** When they express themselves angrily or speak to you with disrespect, reward them by allowing continued discussion. When they do not get their way, and they sulk or pout, don't discipline them. Try hard instead to cheer them up. Distract them. Buy them a treat. Cave in and change your mind. You will send them the message that they are in charge and you fear their disapproval. As the years go on, they will become more and more angry when they do not get their way. After all, you have accidentally sent them the message that they should have it.

25. **Cease a time of chastisement before it has produced humility.** This is probably the greatest cause of exasperated children. Parents attempt to subdue the will through biblical chastisement, but they end each attempt before the child has humbled himself and accepted responsibility for his actions. Many parents fight strong-willed, angry adolescents, because they consistently failed to bring humility through discipline. Each time of chastisement only evokes more and more anger. (See chapter 6, "How to Tell When a Time of Chastisement Is Completed.")

16

SHELTERING CHILDREN

"Kids have to face real life some time—you can't protect them
forever."
*This is a line often spoken by parents who do not understand their
God-given responsibility to oversee and direct their children.*

ACCEPTING VARIABLES AS ABSOLUTES

Most parents love their children. They want what is best for them
and would give their lives to protect them. However, despite their
protective concern, too few parents stop to consider the spiritual
and moral dangers of the day-to-day situations in which they place
their children. They have wrongly considered to be *absolutes* things
like school, youth group, choir, summer camp, sports, friends, the-
ater productions, music, dances, dating, Sunday School, Christian
clubs, etc. None of these are inherently evil, but each puts your children under the authority or influence of someone else—someone
who does not love your children as much as you do, nor will be
held accountable on Judgment Day for them.

Is it possible that one or all of those activities or settings
has more of a corrupting than a redeeming influence on your

children? Could it be that a member of the youth group will introduce your son to drugs, or seduce your daughter at summer camp? Is it possible that your son's rebellious attitude might disappear if you removed him from his school or prohibited him being with certain friends?

These hypothetical possibilities are not offered because this book's agenda is to get you to pull your children out of these activities. They are offered to help you reevaluate those things you have considered to be absolutes. Some of these activities might be completely safe and have no negative impact on the goals of your child training, but then again, they might *all* be dangerous. Too many parents have thwarted their own efforts at training up godly children, because they assumed they needed to send them off to a community program or to a church-sponsored event.

Let us not repeat Israel's parenting mistakes. They were given guidelines for raising their children[1] and were admonished to keep them from intimate association with the pagan inhabitants of the Promised Land.[2] God knew the pagan influence would be so infectious that He commanded Israel to drive out every non-Israelite. Read His warnings in Deuteronomy 8:19–20; Exodus 23:32–33; 34:12; Numbers 33:51–56; and Joshua 23:7,12–13. The book of Judges reveals how every new generation of Israelites grew up and were drawn into idolatry and rebellion against God, because their parents disregarded God's prohibitions and warnings.[3] Learning from Israel's mistakes may save you years of heartache. (Also read Proverbs 13:20; 23:17; 24:1; 1 Corinthians 15:33.)

---

1   Deut. 6:6–9; 11:16–23.

2   Deut. 7:1–6, 16.

3   Judg. 1:27–33; 2:3.

Parents should consider that no traditional American childhood experience absolutely has to happen. They are *variables* in life. The only absolute is that we must raise up offspring who love God and emulate His character. We must chase from our minds the idea that children will only be fulfilled in childhood if they have certain traditional experiences. We must erase the thought that children can only be prepared for "real life" by being immersed in worldly influences and experiencing overwhelming temptation. Israelite children were vulnerable and their parents failed to protect them. We must not repeat Israel's mistakes.

As conscientious parents, we must ask ourselves what good will it do our children to spend multiple hours each week under the influence of those who may corrupt their values or tempt them to sin? Childhood is so brief, why would we want them to spend excessive amounts of time doing something that offers no spiritual value, and does little to bring them to maturity?

If maturity is developed by denying self and responsibly serving others, and immaturity is fed by spending excessive time in self-indulgent activities, why would we want our children to spend multiple hours each week involved in such things? We must evaluate their pursuits and decide if the time and energy required will actually make them mature and prepare them for their adult roles.

What variables have you made into absolutes? Mom, do you really need that job, or do your children need you more? Dad, has greater income become more important than time with your kids? Are you justifying keeping them in that particular school because it is convenient, despite its obvious corrupting influence? If you fear for your son's well-being, because his soccer teammates seem to be having a greater negative influence on him than he is having a positive one on them, who says you have to leave him on the team?

OVER-RELIANCE ON SHELTERING

I want to add an important clarification here: It is possible for parents to depend too heavily upon sheltering their children from moral and spiritual corruption. Sheltering doesn't do anything to give character—it does not transform the human heart—it merely preserves it, temporarily. Sheltering is nothing more than keeping something flammable away from a heat source. Parents who make sheltering a large part of their child rearing are in for a great disappointment.

Sheltering our families is critical for their moral and spiritual purity, but it is possible to become over-dependent on it. Parents can tell if they are in that category, because they say things like, "I am controlling the influences in my children's lives, so I am going to control the outcome." Such words reveal a parent who thinks sheltering gives character.

The truth is that fruitful parenting is more about what we put into our children than what we protect them from. Be certain to spend more time igniting a love for Jesus in your children than sheltering them from the world.

17

BEYOND OBEDIENCE: RAISING CHILDREN WHO LOVE GOD AND OTHERS

Do nothing out of selfish ambition or vain conceit, but in humility consider others better than yourselves. Each of you should look not only to your own interests, but also to the interests of others. Your attitude should be the same as that of Christ Jesus.
—Phil. 2:3–5

THE GOOD THING

Children must learn to honor and obey their parents. As they do, they develop the virtue of self-control, which lays the foundation for maturity, and prepares their hearts to receive moral instruction from their parents.

THE TROUBLING THING

Many parents grasp the importance of raising obedient, respectful children, but fail to understand the significance of raising them to be lovers of God and others. They assume that a self-governing child, raised in the Christian faith, will automatically grow to spiritual maturity as they grow in physical and mental maturity. However, such parents often discover that when their children reach adulthood, they may not continue in the morality or faith that their parents sought to give them. Even more frightening, some parents *are* content with the results of their parenting, but shouldn't be. They are satisfied that their children have grown up and remain active in the church, but these grownup children lack the most important Christian virtue—*love*.

As followers of Christ, we must raise children who not only have the virtue of self-control, but who are lovers of God and true lovers of their families,[1] neighbors,[2] and enemies.[3]

Sadly, many parents do not value love as the highest virtue in their own personal lives, and therefore content themselves with simply raising their children to be obedient. They justify such an approach, insisting Christ taught that those who learn to obey are learning to love. Obedience certainly can be a trait of love,[4] but to subdue our children's wills and then neglect to teach them to love is like building the foundation for a house, and then stopping construction. The foundation is absolutely necessary, but the goal is the house. So, too, obedience and respect, which spring from a subdued self-will, represent important elements of the foundation, but they are just that—foundational elements for the building of love.

Parents, gauge your values. Will you be satisfied if your children are obedient and respectful, serve in church ministries, wear conservative clothes, have neatly groomed hair, and listen only to hymns? These things may be good signs, but not if the children are socially cold and grow up with no concern for the

---

1   Love is proven not by how we treat the needy, but by how we treat our families. (1 Tim. 5:8)

2   Luke 10:29–37.

3   Love is proven not by how we treat our friends, but how we treat those who oppose us. (Matt. 5:46–47)

4   John 14:15: "If you love me, you will obey what I command."

lost or noticeable love for others, not if they are so self-involved that they avoid meeting new people and are not accustomed to reaching out to strangers, or opening their homes to the needy.

Check your goals. Will you be satisfied if your children can quote the entire Westminster Shorter Catechism, are so self-governing that they are able to sit silent and motionless in church for hours at a time, and are so well-behaved that wherever you walk, they remain right by your side? Such self-restrained actions are a good foundation, but may be meaningless if they continually gossip, criticize, and demean others.

Will you be content if your sons wear suits to church and your daughters modest dresses, if they are known to be hard-working and responsible, and they address all adults as Mr. and Mrs.? If so, do not overlook their heart condition that allows them to continually bicker at home, and be unkind to all who offend them.

What if your children are as well-mannered at home as they are in public, and their only flaw is their tendency to point out the shortcomings of others? We are foolish to be happy if our children's only imperfection is their arrogance, for God resists the proud.[5] A well-behaved proud child is useless to his fellow man and just as displeasing to God as a defiant rebel.[6]

---

5   James 4:6.

6   Luke 18:10–14: "Two men went up to the temple to pray, one a Pharisee and the other a tax collector. The Pharisee stood up and prayed about himself: 'God, I thank you that I am not like other men—robbers, evildoers, adulterers—or even like this tax collector. I fast twice a week and give a tenth of all I get.' "But the tax collector stood at a distance. He would not even look up to heaven, but beat his breast and said, 'God, have mercy on me, a sinner.' "I tell you that this man, rather than the other, went home justified before God. For everyone who exalts himself will be humbled, and he who humbles himself will be exalted." See also Matt. 21:31; Mark 2:17; John 9:39–41; 1 Tim. 3:6.

THE REAL THING

We know from Christ's teaching that the highest priority for His followers is that they love God preeminently, and be as devoted to their neighbors as they are to themselves.[7] Therefore, as we rear our children, our chief goal must be to raise them to love God and their neighbors.

The apostle Paul reinforced this when he declared to his spiritual children that the goal of his instruction was not simply that they have right knowledge, but that whatever they learned from him would cause them to love.[8] Quite naturally then, love was the quality he affirmed most often in letters to the churches.[9] Even when he told the Thessalonian church that they loved so well that they didn't need further teaching about it, he still proceeded to instruct them to love more and more.[10] And in Paul's first letter to the church at Corinth, God made it quite clear that no matter what we accomplish or how spiritual we get, if we fail to love, it is worthless.[11]

---

7   Matt. 22:37–39: Jesus replied: "'Love the Lord your God with all your heart and with all your soul and with all your mind.' This is the first and greatest commandment. And the second is like it: 'Love your neighbor as yourself.'"

8   1 Tim. 1:5: "But the goal of our instruction is love from a pure heart and a good conscience and a sincere faith."

9   Eph. 1:15; Phil. 1:9; Col. 1:4–5, 8; 1 Thess. 1:3; 3:6, 12; 4:9–10; 2 Thess. 1:3; Philem. 1:5, 7.

10   1 Thess. 4:9–10: "Now about brotherly love we do not need to write to you, for you yourselves have been taught by God to love each other. And in fact, you do love all the brothers throughout Macedonia. Yet we urge you, brothers, to do so more and more."

11   1 Cor. 13:1–3: "Though I speak with the tongues of men and of angels, but have not love, I have become sounding brass or a clanging cymbal. And though I have the gift of prophecy, and understand all mysteries and all knowledge, and though I have all faith, so that I could remove mountains, but have not love, I am nothing. And though I bestow all my goods to feed the poor, and though I give my body to be burned, but have not love, it profits me nothing."

So, if we raise children who have the ability to speak in the tongues of angels, have the faith to move mountains, perform deeds of self-sacrificing benevolence, and can obey in a flash with total respect, but lack love, we have accomplished *nothing*. Zip. Zero. Nada. Yes, obedient, self-governing children are beautiful and necessary, but if they do not *love*, they lack the quality most dear to the heart of our God.

THE GREATEST THING

Based on the supreme commandment, we know that the greatest thing in parenting is to raise children to love God. The apostle John teaches us that those who love God do so because they first experience His love.[12] We must make it our goal therefore, to somehow convey God's love to our kids. The following four steps should aid any parent in helping their children to grow in love with God.

1. Teach Them the Doctrinal Truth of the Gospel: God Loves Sinners

> But God demonstrates his own love for us in this: While we were still sinners, Christ died for us. Since we have now been justified by his blood, how much more shall we be saved from God's wrath through him! For if, when we were God's enemies, we were reconciled to him through the death of his Son, how much more, having been reconciled, shall we be saved through his life! (Rom. 5:8–10)

> Therefore, I tell you, her many sins have been forgiven—for she loved much. But he who has been forgiven little loves little. (Luke 7:47)

---

12   1 John 4:19: "We love him, because he first loved us."

For us to pass on to our children the Truth that will cause them to grow in love with God, we must first understand it ourselves. When God sent His son as an atoning sacrifice for our sins, it wasn't because we deserved His love. Quite the opposite, we deserved His wrath. God is a righteous and holy judge who saw us not as good, lovable beings deserving of His love and mercy, but as sinners who offended Him. That is what makes Him so wonderful—He loves those who deserve to be *judged*. The gospel is glorious, because it is about God having mercy on His enemies, personally paying off a debt His enemies owed to Him.

When we first call upon Christ we do so because we know we are "sinners" in need of a savior. However, many saved sinners fail to comprehend the depth of mercy they needed from God. They do not see the severity of their sinfulness, so do not appreciate the greatness of God's mercy. As Jesus taught—those who grasp the depth of their sinfulness, will love God all the more.[13]

To love God with all our hearts, we must see that we did not merit the forgiveness Christ's death provided—we deserved the death itself. God hated our wickedness, but poured out His wrath on His innocent son instead of us.

In depicting our sinful condition, God describes our hearts as desperately wicked and deceitful above all things.[14] Until we receive from Him a new nature in salvation,[15] every motive we have is polluted and corrupt.[16] Our best deeds, He says, are like filthy rags.[17] In fact, God is so holy and pure that next to Him, the sun

---

13   Luke 7:47.

14   Jer. 17:9; Job 15:15–16; 25:4-6; Mark 7:20–23; John 2:24–5; Rom. 3:10–18.

15   2 Cor. 5:17.

16   Gen. 6:5; 8:21.

17   Isa. 64:6.

is not bright,[18] and we are like maggots and worms.[19] God sees us as totally depraved sinners,[20] and when Christ sacrificed Himself on the cross, He suffered the wrath God felt toward us in our sins. What love this is! The perfect and pure God of the universe suffered a horrible death for those He counted as enemies. We offend the Righteous Judge and instead of executing sentence upon us, condemning us to eternal punishment, He suffers our death sentence for us. He reaches out and loves the very sinners who deserve His wrath. What a merciful God!

Parents, we must grasp this Truth for ourselves, and pass it on to our children. If they are to fall in love with God, they must understand the depth of the gospel. Here are but a few aspects of His great gift:

- It was *Christ's* actions that reconciled us to God, not *ours*.

  For if, when we were God's enemies, *we were reconciled* to him through the death of his Son, how much more, *having been reconciled*, shall we be saved through his life! (Rom. 5:10)

  All this is from God, *who reconciled us to himself* through Christ and gave us the ministry of reconciliation: 19 that God was reconciling the world to himself in Christ, not counting men's sins against them. And he has committed to us the message of reconciliation. (2 Cor. 5:18–19)

---

18   Job 15:15–16; 25:4–6.

19   Job 25:5–6.

20   Ps. 14:2–3; 51:5; Eccles. 7:29.

> But now *he has reconciled* you by Christ's physical
> body through death to *present you holy* in his
> sight, without blemish and free from accusation.
> (Col. 1:22)

- Christ's death completely took away our sins.[21]

> He did not enter by means of the blood of goats
> and calves; but he entered the Most Holy Place *once
> for all* by his own blood, having obtained eternal
> redemption. (Heb 9:12)

> So Christ was *sacrificed once to take away the sins* of
> many people; and he will appear a second time, not
> to bear sin, but to bring salvation to those who are
> waiting for him. (Heb. 9:28)

> And by that will, we have been made holy through
> the sacrifice of the body of Jesus Christ once for all...
> 17 Then he adds: "Their sins and lawless acts I will
> remember no more." (Heb. 10:10 & 17)

- It was Christ, through his life and death, that made us at
  peace with God – not our consistency.

> Therefore, since we have been justified through faith,
> *we have peace with God through our Lord Jesus Christ.*
> . . . (Rom. 5:1)

- Christ brought us near to God when we were unable to draw
  close to Him on our own.

> But now in Christ Jesus you who once were far away
> *have been brought near* through the blood of Christ.
> (Eph. 2:13)

---

21   John 1:29.

- It is Christ's finished work on the cross that allows us to come boldly into God's presence – not our worthiness.

> Let us therefore *come boldly unto the throne* of grace, that we may obtain mercy, and find grace to help in time of need. (Heb. 4:16)

> *Having* therefore, brethren, *boldness to enter* into the holiest by the blood of Jesus. . . . (Heb. 10:19)

- Our Lord did all our work for us and gave us the task of believing in him.

> Then they asked him, "What must we do to do the works God requires?" 29 Jesus answered, "*The work of God is this: to believe in the one he has sent.*" (John 6:28)

> Now when a man works, his wages are not credited to him as a gift, but as an obligation.[5] However, to the man who does not work but trusts God who justifies the wicked, his faith is credited as righteousness. (Rom. 4:4)

To be contagiously smitten with God is to fully understand what He did to reconcile us to Himself. Pray that you will grasp what it means to be reconciled with God. It will change who you are and give you more to pass onto your children.

2. Teach Them Who God Is—the Most Amazing and Lovable Being Who Has Ever Existed

> And I pray that you, being rooted and established in love, may have power, together with all the saints, to grasp how wide and long and high and deep is the love of Christ, and

to know this love that surpasses knowledge–that you may be filled to the measure of all the fullness of God. (Eph. 3:17–19)

When we truly understand the gospel message, we come to know God as incredibly lovable. Yet, even aside from seeing the mercy revealed on the cross, those who know Him find themselves in awe of Him and enamored with Him. The old expression "to know Him is to love Him" must have started with God. If we want our children to love God, then in the words of author Tedd Tripp, "Dazzle them with God!"[22]

Do you know anyone who is "dazzled" with God? Do you know what that looks like, and do you know what it is about God that dazzles them? One who was enthralled with God was King David—he was thoroughly smitten with Him. So fulfilled was he by his intimate relationship with his Heavenly Father, he once declared, ". . . As the deer pants for streams of water, so my soul pants for you, O God. My soul thirsts for God, for the living God. When can I go and meet with God?"[23] And again, "One thing I ask of the LORD, this is what I seek: that I may dwell in the house of the LORD all the days of my life, to gaze upon the beauty of the LORD and to seek him in his temple."[24]

The longer David got to know God, the more he found Him to be absolutely and totally wonderful.

I have seen you in the sanctuary and beheld your power and your glory. Because your love is better than life, my lips will glorify you. I will praise you as long as I live, and in your name I will lift up my hands. My soul will be satisfied as with

---

22   From the seminar, "Shepherding a Child's Heart."

23   Ps. 42:1–2.

24   Ps. 27:4.

the richest of foods; with singing lips my mouth will praise you. On my bed I remember you; I think of you through the watches of the night. Because you are my help, I sing in the shadow of your wings. My soul clings to you; your right hand upholds me. (Ps. 63:2–8)

David loved God because he appreciated how He rescued and provided him safety in times of trouble.

But I will sing of your strength, in the morning I will sing of your love; for you are my fortress, my refuge in times of trouble. (Psalm 59:16)

From the ends of the earth I call to you, I call as my heart grows faint; lead me to the rock that is higher than I. For you have been my refuge, a strong tower against the foe. I long to dwell in your tent forever and take refuge in the shelter of your wings. (Psalm 61:2–4)

My soul finds rest in God alone; my salvation comes from him. He alone is my rock and my salvation; he is my fortress, I will never be shaken. (Psalm 62:1–2)

David loved God for the wisdom and practical value of His laws.

Oh, how I love your law! I meditate on it all day long. (Psalm 119:97)

Your statutes are wonderful; therefore I obey them. (Psalm 119:129)

I obey your statutes, for I love them greatly. I obey your precepts and your statutes, for all my ways are known to you. (Psalm 119:167–168)

The law of the LORD is perfect, reviving the soul. The statutes of the LORD are trustworthy, making wise the simple. (Psalm 19:7)

David found Him faithful and dependable.

For the word of the LORD is right and true; he is faithful in all he does. (Psalm 33:4)

Your kingdom is an everlasting kingdom, and your dominion endures through all generations. The LORD is faithful to all his promises and loving toward all he has made. (Psalm 145:13)

David was enthralled with God as the Creator.

Come, let us sing for joy to the LORD; let us shout aloud to the Rock of our salvation. Let us come before him with thanksgiving and extol him with music and song. For the LORD is the great God, the great King above all gods. In his hand are the depths of the earth, and the mountain peaks belong to him. The sea is his, for he made it, and his hands formed the dry land. Come, let us bow down in worship, let us kneel before the LORD our Maker; for he is our God and we are the people of his pasture, the flock under his care. (Psalm 95:1–7)

For you created my inmost being; you knit me together in my mother's womb. I praise you because I am fearfully and wonderfully made; your works are wonderful, I know that full well. (Psalm 139:13–14)

David was in awe of God's omnipresence.

> Where can I go from your Spirit? Where can I flee from your presence? If I go up to the heavens, you are there; if I make my bed in the depths, you are there. (Psalm 139:7–8)

David was amazed by God's omniscience.

> O LORD, you have searched me and you know me. You know when I sit and when I rise; you perceive my thoughts from afar. You discern my going out and my lying down; you are familiar with all my ways. Before a word is on my tongue you know it completely, O LORD. You hem me in—behind and before; you have laid your hand upon me. Such knowledge is too wonderful for me, too lofty for me to attain. (Psalm 139:1–6)

David revered God for His incredible power.

> The mountains melt like wax before the LORD, before the Lord of all the earth. (Psalm 97:5)

> How awesome are your deeds! So great is your power that your enemies cringe before you. (Psalm 66:3)

> I have seen you in the sanctuary and beheld your power and your glory. Because your love is better than life, my lips will glorify you. (Psalm 63:2–3)

> Great is the LORD and most worthy of praise; his greatness no one can fathom. One generation will commend your works to another; they will tell of your mighty acts. They will speak of the glorious splendor of your majesty, and I will meditate on your wonderful works. They will tell of the power of your awesome works, and I will proclaim your great deeds. (Psalm 145:3–6)

David feared God for His great authority.

> My flesh trembles in fear of you; I stand in awe of your laws. (Psalm 119:120)

> You alone are to be feared. Who can stand before you when you are angry? (Psalm 76:7)

> Who knows the power of your anger? For your wrath is as great as the fear that is due you. (Psalm 90:11)

> If you, O LORD, kept a record of sins, O Lord, who could stand? 4 But with you there is forgiveness; therefore you are feared. (Psalm 130:3–4)

> Taste and see that the LORD is good; blessed is the man who takes refuge in him. Fear the LORD, you his saints, for those who fear him lack nothing . . . Come, my children, listen to me; I will teach you the fear of the LORD. (Psalm 34:8–11)

This chapter does not allow the space needed to help the reader discover all that is wonderful about our Heavenly Father, but there is a path we can walk to meet Him. God makes a simple promise that He always fulfills. If we seek Him *with all our hearts* He will reveal Himself to us.[25] We must spend time in the Word with a hungry, humble heart, praying that there we will encounter God. If we are to help our children find God irresistible, we must know Him deeply ourselves.

---

25   Jer. 29:13–14: "And you will seek Me and find Me, when you search for Me with all your heart. And I will be found by you,' declares the LORD . . . "

3. Model for Them Love for God

> I have set you an example that you should do as I have done for you. (John 13:15)

> Set an example for the believers in speech, in life, in love, in faith and in purity. (1 Tim. 4:12)

If you want your children to love God, then it will be important that you teach them to love Him by your example. The saying, "the most important things in life are *caught* not *taught*," is particularly true with our children. What we *do* teaches them more than what we *say*. Our words, in fact, may be of little influence, if they are not matched by a genuine heart of love for God.

For the glory of God and for the sake of our children, we must make it our goal to love the Lord with all our heart, mind, soul, and strength. It is good to employ the best biblical parenting principles, but proper discipline impacts primarily our children's *behavior*. It is a parent's sincere love for God that will impact their souls most. We need both.

A problem faced by some parents is that the "love for God" they model doesn't look to their children like love at all. From listening to their parents the children perceive the Christian life to be a loveless, joyless, preoccupation with *looking* like a Christian and avoiding bad stuff. Certainly, a critical aspect of walking with Christ is throwing off everything that hinders and the sin that entangles,[26] as well as avoiding harmful influences.[27] However, if it appears to our children that our Christian life is drudgery and a burden, and our dominant concern is with what we must *avoid*

---

26 Heb. 12:1.

27 2 Cor. 6:17–7:1; James 1:27.

and what we *don't do*, we must ask ourselves—will they want that? *We* don't even really want that for ourselves!

Parents—are your children drawn to your Jesus or is your "religion" just a burden they feel heaped upon them? Remember, Jesus cautioned the Jewish leaders against loading people down with burdens they could not carry.[28]

The Christian life is not simply about *not* doing bad stuff. It is not even about doing good in order to gain God's approval. A walk with Christ is a life of joyful thankfulness. It is daily enjoying God's love and mercy, and doing good for Him because He accepts us—not because we are striving to get accepted.[29]

When Jesus called followers to Himself, He said, "Come to me, all you who are weary and burdened, and I will give you rest. Take my yoke upon you and learn from me, for I am gentle and humble in heart, and you will find rest for your souls. For my yoke is easy and my burden is light."[30] The life Jesus has for His people is one of beauty. If our walk with Him is a burden, and our souls have no rest, we are obviously missing what it means to live a life of love for God.

For our sake and for the sake of our children, may we all pursue what it means to be loved by God and love Him in return.

---

28   Luke 11:46.

29   Rom. 5:10: "For if, when we were God's enemies, we were reconciled to him through the death of his Son, how much more, having been reconciled, shall we be saved through his life!"
Rom. 2:4: "Or do you show contempt for the riches of his kindness, tolerance and patience, not realizing that God's kindness leads you toward repentance?"

30   Matt. 11:28.

4. Convey to Them the Love of God by Loving Them

> Dear friends, let us love one another, for love comes from God. Everyone who loves has been born of God and knows God. Whoever does not love does not know God, because God is love . . . And so we know and rely on the love God has for us. God is love. Whoever lives in love lives in God, and God in him. (1 John 4:7–8, 16)

Philip, the disciple, once requested of Jesus, "Lord, show us the Father . . . " To which he received the reply, "Don't you know me, Philip, even after I have been among you such a long time? Anyone who has seen me has seen the Father. How can you say, 'Show us the Father.'"[31] Jesus's statement was clearly an affirmation of His deity, but was also an illustration of how one person can be a reflection of another. So, too, as children of God, we can reflect Him and His love to our own children.

Have you ever stopped to consider that it was love that made Jesus attractive to sinners and allowed Him to influence them? He spoke against sin, but He still drew sinners to himself. He hated evil, and preached for holiness, but those sinners who heard Him, somehow knew He accepted them. In fact, so great and evident was His merciful love that He became known as the "friend of sinners."[32] If our children receive our complete love and acceptance, they will be more drawn to us and to our God.

Jesus's interaction with the woman at the well was a beautiful example of the power of acceptance.[33] He met her at the well outside of Samaria and set out to win her heart. He revealed to

---

31 John 14:8–9.

32 Matt. 11:19; 9:10–11; Luke 7:34; 15:1–2.

33 John 4.

her that He knew she had had five husbands and was now living with a man in fornication. He pronounced no judgment—just stated the facts. This exposure of her failings embarrassed her, prompting her to mildly attack Him. He didn't return her attacks, but calmly persisted in pursuing her heart. She was completely undone by His acceptance. She found that this one, who saw her for who she was, was *safe* with her failings. The operative word here is *safe*. That's what acceptance does—it says, "I see you in your weakness and sins, and like you anyway." I may want you to be better than you are, but you don't have to be better for me to accept you." Jesus accepted her in her weakness, not because she was good, but because He was good.

Zacchaeus, the despised tax collector, was a classic example of a sinner who was transformed by the love and acceptance of Christ. There he was up that tree, trying to get a good look at Jesus, when suddenly Jesus caught a glimpse of him. Christ responded by declaring, "Zacchaeus, come down immediately. I must stay at your house today." That was all it took. Zacchaeus's heart was changed. He instantly made a commitment to share his wealth with the needy and repay anyone from whom he had stolen.[34] *Christ's* love caused *him* to love.

Have you ever noticed that you are drawn to people who accept you, and you tend to avoid people who don't? And have you noticed that you listen more to people who have affection for you, and tend to resist those who are angry or annoyed with you? Has it occurred to you that your children may be just like you?

Do you want your children to love your Jesus? Then it will be important that you love them with the same love God has for you. You will be attractive and they will be more inclined to want

---

34   Luke 19:1–10.

to know your Jesus. For the sake of our children, let us strive to understand what it means that God loves and accepts us even before we have grown perfectly into the image of His son.

God loves me, but does He *like* me?

All Christians believe that God loves them—it is the basis of the gospel message.[35] In my travels I have surveyed people around the world and have found that although they believe God loves them, the vast majority feel He doesn't *like* them all that much. In fact, most are convinced He is rather disappointed in them, so they live under a cloud of His disapproval.

What this reveals is that most of God's children are not happy with themselves, so assume their heavenly Father is unhappy with them as well. They strive in their Christian lives hoping to eventually merit God's approval, but it seems too elusive. He is the perpetual Father in the sky with high standards, who is too hard to please and rarely smiles in their direction. As a result, the majority of God's children live discouraged, powerless lives.

It is a dangerous theology to believe that God loves us, but won't *like* us until we are more consistent in our walks with Him. It ignores that God set His affection on us back when we were His enemies, before we were His beloved children.[36] Believing that our Heavenly Father *loves*, but does not *like* us infers He does not accept us as weak, fleshly beings and is postponing acceptance

---

35   John 3:16.

36   But God demonstrates his own love for us in this: While we were still sinners, Christ died for us. 9 Since we have now been justified by his blood, how much more shall we be saved from God's wrath through him! 10 For if, when we were God's enemies, we were reconciled to him through the death of his Son, how much more, having been reconciled, shall we be saved through his life! Rom 5:8-10.

until we achieve greater maturity. Unfortunately, as parents, we transfer this exact parenting approach to our children.

We may love our kids, but we are emotionally taxed by the challenge they present, so we tend to relate with them like they are problems to be fixed or endured, especially when they are in adolescence.

We may not even be aware that we do not like our kids, because we care so much about them and are so committed to their good. However, our kids sense it when we don't like them. They feel it every time we interact with them – by our countenance, our tone of voice, or the suspicious manner in which we question them.

We are their parents, which means they look to us for approval more than to anyone else. If by the time they reach adolescence, they do not feel they are our delight, they will begin looking elsewhere for value and significance.

If we want to influence our children beyond their younger years, we had better learn what it means that God accepts us for who we are at whatever stage of growth we have attained. We must know and rejoice that we can walk into His presence at any time and be greeted with a smile, not because we are finally good, but because *He* is good.

If you want to be able to accept your children when they are still miles from maturity, you must enjoy what it means that you can approach God's throne of grace with boldness – not because you have earned the privilege, but because *He* has.[37]

The more you walk in awareness of God's love and what He accomplished on the cross, the easier it will become to accept your children in all their weaknesses.

---

37   Heb. 10:19: Having therefore, brethren, boldness to enter into the holiest by the blood of Jesus; Heb. 4:16: Let us therefore come boldly unto the throne of grace, that we may obtain mercy, and find grace to help in time of need.

THE SECOND GREATEST THING

Christ taught that next to loving God, loving *others* should be the Christian's greatest pursuit.[38] Parents, therefore, must teach their children from infancy that they are to love others as themselves. Those who make this a foundational goal of their child training will set their children dead center on the path to maturity and will establish in them the basis for respect of others.

If we want to teach our children to be as devoted to their siblings, neighbors, and enemies as they are to themselves, there are several steps we can take.

1. Be Certain You Are First Filled Full with the Love of Christ

Just like a dry well has no refreshment to offer, we will be unable to love others if we have not first drunk deeply from God's spring. He is the source of all our compassion. He is the power behind our selfless care. Daily we must go to God to refresh ourselves in His love for us, and this love we must give to others.

As I hope I have communicated thus far, we can never be content that we grasp fully the love of Christ. For God's sake and for our sake, let alone for our children's sake, let us embark on a journey to discover and drink of the love of God.

> . . . And I pray that you, being rooted and established in love, may have power, together with all the saints, to grasp how wide and long and high and deep is the love of Christ, and to know this love that surpasses knowledge--that you may be filled to the measure of all the fullness of God. (Eph. 3:17-19)

---

38   Matt. 22:36–39; Phil. 2:5–8.

2. Study the Scriptures to Understand Love in All of Its Facets

Our Lord was the picture of love. To grow in our knowledge of love, we must study all that He taught and all that He did. The Greek word used to describe His love is agape, which conveys quite a depth of meaning:

- Love is a commitment based on a decision of the will, and not on emotion. It is not earned or deserved, but is unconditional. This means that we are never free to withhold love based on what another does. It is for this reason that Christ calls us to be gracious and merciful toward those who offend us, including users, abusers, and false accusers.

> But I tell you who hear me: Love your enemies, do good to those who hate you, bless those who curse you, pray for those who mistreat you. If someone strikes you on one cheek, turn to him the other also. If someone takes your cloak, do not stop him from taking your tunic. Give to everyone who asks you, and if anyone takes what belongs to you, do not demand it back. (Luke 6:27–30)

> Do not repay anyone evil for evil. Be careful to do what is right in the eyes of everybody. If it is possible, as far as it depends on you, live at peace with everyone. Do not take revenge, my dear friends, but leave room for God's wrath, for it is written: "It is mine to avenge; I will repay," says the Lord. On the contrary: "If your enemy is hungry, feed him; if he is thirsty, give him something to drink. In doing this, you will heap burning coals on his head." Do not be overcome by evil, but overcome evil with good. (Rom. 12:17–21)

- Love is proven by sacrifice. We may have great affection for others, and even maintain a commitment to them, but if we are unwilling to inconvenience ourselves, we are missing a key ingredient of true love. Loving without cost may not be love at all. The sacrifices of love may be physical, emotional, or mental, and may include the yielding of personal rights.

> Greater love has no one than this, that he lay down his life for his friends. (John 15:13)[39]

> This is how we know what love is: Jesus Christ laid down his life for us. And we ought to lay down our lives for our brothers. (1 John 3:16)

> Your attitude should be the same as that of Christ Jesus: Who, being in very nature God, did not consider equality with God something to be grasped, but made himself nothing, taking the very nature of a servant, being made in human likeness. And being found in appearance as a man, he humbled himself and became obedient to death—even death on a cross! (Phil. 2:5–8)

- Love is not only sacrificial, but is *selfless* in its motives. It gives because the other needs, and not because it wants a return on the investment. It does not give to get. True love remains constant because it is given without strings and is not dependent on demands or expectations. The whole concept of loving another to get one's own needs met is entirely self-centered. Christ gave of Himself not because He had need of us, but because we had need of Him.

> We who are strong ought to bear with the failings of the weak and not to please ourselves. Each of us should please his neighbor for his good, to build him up. For even Christ did not please himself . . . (Rom. 15:1–3)

---

39   Also John 10:11; Rom. 5:8.

[Love] . . . is not self-seeking . . . (1 Cor. 13:5)

But when you give a banquet, invite the poor, the crippled, the lame, the blind, and you will be blessed. Although they cannot repay you, you will be repaid at the resurrection of the righteous. (Luke 14:13–14)

Nobody should seek his own good, but the good of others. (1 Cor. 10:24)

Even as I try to please everybody in every way. For I am not seeking my own good but the good of many, so that they may be saved. (1 Cor. 10:33)

- Love cares for others so seeks to understand and relate with them. It is because we care that we are willing to forego what is comfortable to us, and put ourselves in another's place, either literally or empathetically.

For this reason he had to be made like his brothers in every way, in order that he might become a merciful and faithful high priest in service to God, and that he might make atonement for the sins of the people. Because he himself suffered when he was tempted, he is able to help those who are being tempted. (Heb. 2:17–18)

For we do not have a high priest who is unable to sympathize with our weaknesses, but we have one who has been tempted in every way, just as we are—yet was without sin. (Heb. 4:15)

Brothers, if someone is caught in a sin, you who are spiritual should restore him gently. But watch yourself, or you also may be tempted. Carry each other's burdens, and in this way you will fulfill the law of Christ. (Gal. 6:1–2)

- Love is empty if it is void of action. Warm words can be powerful, but just as faith is dead without works,[40] so also is love. Jesus taught that for love to be valid, it must be expressed through our service of others.

> Not so with you. Instead, whoever wants to become great among you must be your servant, and whoever wants to be first must be your slave—just as the Son of Man did not come to be served, but to serve, and to give his life as a ransom for many." (Matt. 20:26–28)[41]

> Now that I, your Lord and Teacher, have washed your feet, you also should wash one another's feet. (John 13:14)

> If anyone has material possessions and sees his brother in need but has no pity on him, how can the love of God be in him? Dear children, let us not love with words or tongue but with actions and in truth. (1 John 3:17–18)

- The love God has for us is outlined in the thirteenth chapter of 1 Corinthians. To understand His beautiful love will increase our appreciation of Him, as well as empower us to better love others and equip us to teach our children.

> Love is patient, love is kind. It does not envy, it does not boast, it is not proud. It does not dishonor others, it is not self-seeking, it is not easily angered, it keeps no record of wrongs. Love does not delight in evil but rejoices with the truth. It always protects,

---

40   James 2:14–18.

41   Also Matt. 23:11; Luke 22:25–27.

always trusts, always hopes, always perseveres. Love never fails . . . (1 Cor. 13:4–8)

3. Cultivate Love Relationships with Your Children

If we want our children to love us or care for others, it is imperative that they enjoy our love and acceptance. They are no different from us—when we are loved by those important to us, it is more natural to feel love for others.[42] Enjoying the love and affection of parents not only fosters love, but can produce a security and contentedness that actually reduces sibling rivalry. Homes in which children enjoy love become more peaceful with one another.

Before our children reach adolescence it is important that our love relationship with them becomes their strongest motivation for doing what is right. If they reach their teen years and the predominant means of motivating them is *threat of consequence,* we may still have their cooperation, but they are on the road to becoming prodigals. Fear of punishment can motivate behavior change, but will not build trust relationships.

With that in mind, consider the following ways to express love and cultivate trust relationships with your children.

> **a. Accept your children.** Accept them for who they presently are at the level of maturity they have achieved. Note that I didn't say be *content* with their growth, I said *accept* them. Our parental goals will still include influencing them toward God, good character, and maturity, but our children must know it is not their level of maturity that merits our smile. Stop and ponder this, please!

---

42   We love because he first loved us. 1 John 4:19.

As Christians, we try to live by God's standards and seek to hold our children to those standards as well. Unfortunately, in our efforts to spiritually groom our kids, we are tempted to withhold our approval when they don't perform. We don't want them to think they are okay when we are not content with them. We send that message by our tone, our words, and our countenance. Our children desperately need to know we accept and like them, whether they meet the standard yet or not.

- They are who they are. You may not like their immature values, but those values reflect who they actually are at this stage of their life. Your constant vocal disapproval or looks of disappointment will not likely change them—only make them hide their true feelings.

- Do not postpone showing acceptance until they achieve your standard. That may not come before they grow up and move out.

- Many middle-aged adults still crave their parents' approval. Do you want your children to be your age and still be waiting for you to say, "I'm proud of you"? Do you want for them what you may be experiencing with your parents?

- Listen to yourself—do you communicate to them that you are never completely pleased, satisfied, or content with them or their efforts? Is it possible your careful scrutinizing has left them feeling that they can never measure up, like they can never succeed? Have you led them to believe they are a big disappointment to you?

- Consider that your adolescent may be resistant to your leadership, not because they watched bad movies or spent time with questionable friends, but because they feel so rejected by you that they have given up trying to please you. They feel hurt by you.

- Consider that many kids, who fail to find their parents' acceptance, will welcome it from the first group or individual who offers it. They will then begin to adopt the values of the new ones who accept them.

- Remember that we are drawn to those who like us, but have little time for those who continually criticize us. Your children are just like you.

b. Express affection to your children. It is within human nature to need tender affection, and those who cultivate it find it can be a powerful aspect of family bonding.[43]

- Show physical affection to them. If you feel physical affection is not natural for you, because your parents never touched you while you were growing up, your resistance is understandable. Expressing affection may be difficult for you, but you must repent. Deny yourself and your own feelings of discomfort, and give your children what they need. God Himself is a nurturing God[44] and wants us to be like Him.

- Eliminate that suspicious, scrutinizing look with which you typically greet your children and discipline yourself to smile at them. You love them, so why don't you let it leak out through your teeth! None of us responds well to someone who communicates continual mistrust and suspicion. May your countenance

---

43 Rom 2:4: Or do you show contempt for the riches of his kindness, tolerance and patience, not realizing that God's kindness leads you toward repentance? (Also 1 John 4:19)

44 1 Thess. 2:7: but we were gentle among you, like a mother caring for her little children.
Isa. 66:13a: As a mother comforts her child, so will I comfort you ... (Also John 13:23, 25)

become inviting![45] A suspicious scowl is like a sign on a store that says CLOSED: OUT OF BUSINESS. A smile says: OPEN FOR BUSINESS AND EVERYTHING'S ON SPECIAL!

Affirm your children when they do well. Express to them that you knew they would succeed. Listen to yourself: do you correct them more than you affirm them?

c. See them through the eyes of God. Fortunately for us, God does not look only upon the outside, but sees us as His beloved adopted children with new natures. Although we may fall into old habits associated with our former way of life, we are not our old self.[46]

- Our children each have a fleshly nature, but that nature is not their identity and neither is their behavior. If they identify themselves with Christ then they have new identities as God's children.[47]

- Christ accepted and blessed random children, with no regard for their behavior or what they had done in their lives. Some of the children he received could have been little monsters, but he blessed them all alike. Our children deserve the same from us.

---

45   Prov. 16:15: When a king's face brightens, it means life; his favor is like a rain cloud in spring.
Mark 10:21a: Jesus looked at him and loved him...

46   1 Cor. 6:9-11, 19-20.

47   2 Cor. 5:16 Therefore from now on we recognize no man according to the flesh; even though we have known Christ according to the flesh, yet now we know Him thus no longer. 17 Therefore if any man is in Christ, he is a new creature; the old things passed away; behold, new things have come. (Also 1 Sam. 16:7; 1 Kings 8:39; 1 Chron. 28:9)

- Mark 10:13: People were bringing little children to Jesus to have him touch them, but the disciples rebuked them.[14] When Jesus saw this, he was indignant. He said to them, "Let the little children come to me, and do not hinder them, for the kingdom of God belongs to such as these.[15] I tell you the truth, anyone who will not receive the kingdom of God like a little child will never enter it."[16] And he took the children in his arms, put his hands on them and blessed them. (Matt. 18:1-6)

- When they are in need of correction, speak to your children with hope and expectancy. Use phrases like: *"This is not like you..." "You're an honest boy..." "I think you'll make the right choice."* Note the difference between the following two approaches:

"JOHNNY, YOU'VE BEEN MEAN TO YOUR SISTER AGAIN AND I WON'T TOLERATE IT!" or...

"Johnny, I know you love your sister. Tell me how you failed to show it just now, and then tell me what would have been a kinder way to respond."

Many parents who have affectionate relationships with their children assume their children feel accepted. If that is you—be careful. Do not mistake affection for acceptance. Affection can be simply a tender manner and a caring touch—something that even rebellious children crave. Acceptance says, "Although you fall short, I still like you as you are now." Make it your top goal to accept your children at whatever their stage of maturity—just as God accepts you.

PRACTICAL TIPS FOR RAISING LOVING CHILDREN[48]

As I have attempted to communicate, the best way to raise loving children is to create a climate of love in the home. Loving people tend to raise loving children. As a rule of life, love is *caught* more than it is taught. Nonetheless, from the time they are born, we must reinforce our example by elevating love as their life purpose.

1. Emphasize to them throughout their day that loving and serving others is our supreme goal. Evaluate all their social and moral decisions from the standpoint of love.

2. Make frequent opportunities for the family to serve others, i.e., looking after widows or single moms, visiting convalescent hospitals, volunteering at the local Crisis Pregnancy Center, etc.

3. Encourage the children to surprise their siblings by secretly serving them, i.e., doing their chores for them, making their beds, etc.

4. Make the absence of love the issue of every childish dispute. When children are in conflict, do not just rebuke them for fighting, but admonish them for *not loving*. Don't ask them, "Who started it?" Ask them each how have they failed to love the other. Emphasize to them that in any conflict, the one who loves first is the one who wins.

5. Frequently fill their hearts with your loving affection. Since a fresh dose of God's love fills the heart of a new believer with love for others,[49] consider that bickering children may respond powerfully to a moment of strong fatherly affection, i.e., a group hug which does not end until the little ones are laughing and affectionate.

---

48   Adapted from my seminar, "The Delightful Family."

49   1 John 4:19.

6. Pray with them about it, but don't wait until they are mad at their siblings. Every time you pray, including bedtime and meals, ask God to show them creative ways to love others.

7. Read storybooks or make up bedtime stories about children who are kind and compassionate servants.

8. Give them greater affirmation when you see them love and serve than when they hit a homerun. When they love and serve, allow them to hear you brag to others about it.

9. Do not permit *any* unkind words in your family, i.e., no derogatory names, no making fun, no teasing, or belittling of any kind.

10. Model service and kind speech in your marriage. Many have said that the best way for children to learn to love is to be around two parents loving each other.

RESTORING LOST LOVE AND AFFECTION IN A FAMILY
(Particularly with Adolescent-aged Children)

Restoring Lost Love

1. Forgive them. If you carry unrelenting resentment toward any of your children, it is imperative that you clean their slate and give them a fresh start—not just now, but on an ongoing basis. Your resentment will not go unfelt by them or without consequence. Abiding frustration is the fastest way to lose the heart of a child and insure you will raise up a troubled adult.

- Forgive them for existing. If you find yourself continually upset with your children, is it just because they were born and you weren't or aren't ready to be a parent? Might it be because motherhood has kept you from the career you could have had? Is it because their training and care demands so much time, and seems to intrude on your life? If so, own your self-centeredness and renounce it. Choose your children over you. During this season of life, your children do not interrupt your life—they and their training *are* your life. For now you have nothing better to do than be a parent. Yes, you have to make dinner, change the oil in the car, and get ready for meetings, but your children do not need to receive a look of frustration every time their behavior requires your attention.

- Give them the mercy you would like for yourself. Are you impatient with them because they remind you of someone you don't like—*yourself*, perhaps? Is it that you know your own heart, so judge their hearts and read into their motives only evil intentions? If so, recognize it and have the same mercy on them that you would like from God. They are human and so will have bad motives for their actions at times, but immediate anger at their nature will not give them proper motivation to change.

Be kind and compassionate to one another, forgiving each other, just as in Christ God forgave you. Eph. 4:32

Therefore judge nothing before the appointed time; wait till the Lord comes. He will bring to light what is hidden in darkness and will expose the motives of men's hearts. At that time each will receive his praise from God. 1 Cor. 4:5

- Is one of your children more challenging than the others? Do you react to him more sternly than his siblings? When you call your children's names is there one that has an exclamation mark at the end of it? If so, it is time to remove it. None of us are drawn to someone who is always angry with us. You must stop before you demoralize and alienate them!

- Don't bring up old offenses and repeatedly scold them for them. You don't need to cite their past failures to prove to them there is a pattern. Continually listing off their past sins will only dishearten them. Just as you need fresh starts from God, they need them from you.

Do not call to mind the former things, Or ponder things of the past. Isa. 43:18

If you, O LORD, kept a record of sins, O Lord, who could stand? Ps. 130:3

Then he adds: "Their sins and lawless acts I will remember no more." Heb. 10:17

[Love] . . . keeps no record of wrongs. 1 Cor. 13:5

- Give them continued fresh starts. Don't think the worst of them, continually guessing their motives to be evil. Love hopes the best.[50] Give them the benefit of the doubt.

- Remember that abiding bitterness will destroy you and them. We are warned in Hebrews 12:15 to be careful ". . . that *no bitter root grows up to cause trouble and defile many.*" Unresolved anger will color all of your parenting and create a negative climate in your home. Your frustration may intimidate your children into compliance, but they will only comply when you are around, and will long for the day that they can escape the home.

"In your anger do not sin": Do not let the sun go down while you are still angry, 27 and do not give the devil a foothold. Eph. 4:26-27

---

50   1 Cor. 13:7.

- Do not justify your anger. Coercion with rage is a fleshly effort to achieve a spiritual end. We imagine that our children will see our anger and say to themselves, *"Oh, my, what have I done to drive my otherwise sane mother so crazy. I should stop and examine myself."* Yet, most people, when they are being verbally assaulted, do not think selfless thoughts like that. They are too terrified, so are distracted with thoughts of survival and self-preservation. Your anger is not only useless, but is actually destructive, alienating your children and minimizing your influence on them.

For the wrath of man does not produce the righteousness of God. James 1:20

- If you realize that you have allowed yourself to use anger as a motivational tool, go to your family and ask forgiveness of them.

Therefore, if you are offering your gift at the altar and there remember that your brother has something against you, 24 leave your gift there in front of the altar. First go and be reconciled to your brother; then come and offer your gift. Matt. 5:23-24

- Remember that child training is a process. There is no reason to be angry with a child whose training is not yet complete, particularly if you have been training them inadequately. There is especially no reason to be angry with a child that you have trained to ignore you by constantly repeating your instructions and coddling them with multiple warnings. Don't forget that self-absorbed children are typically that way, because a parent has indulged them and fed their narcissism.

The most dangerous thing about angry parents is that they misrepresent who God is to their children. They may tell their kids that God is merciful and loving, but as the primary authority figures in their lives they are modeling that God is anything but tender and patient. Children in such a home typically grow up with a warped view of God. They see Him as harsh, explosive, difficult to please, and hard to approach. If they even bother to stay in the church, they will likely have a legalistic faith that will leave them feeling constantly unworthy of God. Without intending to, angry parents model who they see God to be. The best thing we can do as parents, let alone as Christians, is come to know God for who He *really* is. It will change who we are on the inside—not just what we do.

2. Treat them with kindness. Jesus's command, "Do unto others as you would have them do unto you" applies first to family members. This applies particularly to our children whether they are behaving or not.

- Whenever you look at them, be wary of displaying an expression of suspicion, mistrust, or exasperation on your face. Don't save your smiles for when you watch them sleep. Let them see your love in your countenance.

- Be careful of communicating to them that they are a big disappointment because they fail to keep your standard. Not only should you avoid constant statements of how they have let you down, but be wary sending subtle messages of displeasure, Whenever they blow it, don't blame yourself in front of them, saying something like, "I'm such a failure as a parent. I haven't trained my kids to do something so basic!" Sounds humble, but they know you are really attacking them.

- Don't believe you are kind just because you never call

your children bad names. If they hear you call *yourself* bad names when you make mistakes, they will assume you feel the same way toward them.

- Do not compare them to their better-behaved siblings. Yes, it might seem an effective means of clarifying your standards, but they will grow to resent the siblings to which they are compared.

- Don't raise your voice to them. (Unless you're simply trying to be heard over the noise of a locomotive.) In my personal surveys of children, the vast majority have told me that the most despised, ineffective form of discipline is yelling and scolding. Children can handle calm chastisement or firm correction, but their open hearts cannot handle demeaning words from the very people they look to for affirmation and value.

3. Listen to them.

- At all ages, but particularly as they approach adolescence, give them opportunities to share their heart with you. Bedtime is a perfect time to let them open up. In fact, at bedtime most children will are ripe for serious dialogue—they'll do anything if it means they don't have to go to sleep.

- When they do open up and share their feelings or dreams, listen to them without immediately giving them the correction you think they need. Be someone with whom they are not afraid to share their heart. For example, if your eleven-year-old tells you he wants to save up his money to buy a certain new plaything that you consider an unwise use money, he won't respond well to a lecture on investing foolishly in this world. Values come out of the heart and reveal who a person is.[51] A parent who offers immediate correction every time his child reveals his immature values will eventually discover that child pulling away.

- If the values you hear are immature, don't think you will change their values by simply telling them their values are bad. Instead, devise a plan to nurture the heart that expressed those values.

- When they open up and entrust you with their heart, be trustworthy with it. None of us is willing to risk sharing vulnerable feelings with someone who will attack us with what we share. What they confess about their personal struggles one day, don't use as ammo against them the next.

- To help them open up and entrust their heart to you, it might help them see that you are human too and have your own struggles. It therefore might help them lower their defenses if you share with them weaknesses or struggles you have had in your own life.

Parents, just as God does not intend that the Christian life be burdensome,[52] neither should our parenting. If we are weighed down just trying to survive our children, or if we daily struggle just to tolerate them, we are falling short of God's calling for us. We will always be miserable and our children will not easily be trained. God does not want us just to endure our kids or merely put up with them—He wants us to aggressively love them! There is a vast difference. When we properly love our children, God

---

51   Matt. 12:34b ...For out of the abundance of the heart the mouth speaks.

52   Matt. 11:29–30: "Take my yoke upon you and learn from me, for I am gentle and humble in heart, and you will find rest for your souls. For my yoke is easy and my burden is light."

is glorified and our families reap great blessings. Remember, as Jesus told His followers—when we obey His commandment to love, our joy will be full.[53]

---

53 John 15:10–12: "If you obey my commands, you will remain in my love, just as I have obeyed my Father's commands and remain in his love. I have told you this so that my joy may be in you and that your joy may be complete. My command is this: Love each other as I have loved you."

18

GETTING A FRESH START

Because of the Lord's great love we are not consumed, for his compassions never fail. They are new every morning
—Lamentation 3:22–23

Sometimes when parents reach the conclusion of this book, they are aggravated at themselves or their children. They feel convicted that they have been slack in their parenting and are convinced that their children have gotten away with too much. Has that happened to you? Are you now determined to change things at home? Are you feeling intense and ready for action? Good, but be careful! Before you attempt to change your parenting, first consider the following thoughts:

- Plan a strategy with your spouse.

  Before you go into action, discuss your plans with your mate. If possible, both parents should read this book before one begins implementing anything new. If the children sense there is disharmony between parents, they will play them one against the other.

- Call a family meeting.

  In order to begin implementing proper training, it is important that parents call a meeting with their children to explain the changes that will be occurring in the way the home is run. Make sure they understand the new standards and the consequences for violations. That way they do not become resentful for suddenly being held to new standards without forewarning. They know exactly what is happening, why it is happening, and the kinds of changes they should expect.

- Ask their forgiveness.

  It will be important to begin your meeting by apologizing for failing with your parenting in the past. You have not properly prepared them for maturity, and asking their forgiveness is in order. This will give you a fresh start and establish the basis for the forthcoming changes.

- Warn them of possible inconsistencies.

  Be sure to tell them that as you are relearning your job, you may have blind spots, and therefore may not notice every time they violate a new rule. Warn them that they are not to interpret your lack of action to mean that the new standard is now off.

- Go slow and watch your anger!

  I want to restate what I said in the preface. Keep in mind that our children are a product of our training, whether by intent or neglect. They are only the way they are because we have not yet finished their training. If the children are not learning fast enough, and the training does not seem to be working, then it is time to look for blind spots in our approach, and not time for greater harshness. Children respond best to alert, loving, consistent discipline—not to angry, "don't mess with me, kid" parenting.

- Remember, "untraining" is not easy.

  The repentant parent must remember that the enforcement of new rules can be difficult, because half of the training will be *undoing* the negative training you have done thus far.

- Plan for the possibility of several intense days of frequent chastisement.

  Some children submit easily, but others enjoy being in charge and may not so willingly release control of the home. They must learn right away, however, that you mean business. You may even consider limiting outside commitments for several days or taking a few days off from work, so you can devote yourself fully to consistent discipline.

To summarize a few ideas from chapter 17, keep in mind that most of us find it easier to follow the leadership of one who likes us. Your children must *know* of your affection for them. Affirm your children for their successes, do not always think the worst of them, and speak hopefully to them. Watch your countenance. Do your children see you scowling suspiciously at them every time they walk into the room? Scowling communicates to them mistrust—that you assume the worst of them. It is highly unmotivating to please someone who thinks the worst of you. Discipline yourself to greet your kids with a smile. You *do* love your children, so let it leak out through your teeth. You may be amazed how differently they respond to you.

Thank you for choosing to read

CHILD TRAINING TIPS

If you enjoyed this book, we hope that you will tell your friends and family. There are many ways to spread the word:

Share your thoughts on Facebook, your blog, or Tweet "You should read #CHILDTRAININGTIPS by Reb Bradley // @worldnetdaily Consider using the book in a book group or small group setting. Send a copy to someone you know who would benefit from reading this book.

Write a review online at Amazon.com or BN.com
Subscribe to WND at www.wnd.com
Visit the WND Superstore at superstore.wnd.com

 WND Books

PRESENTS

The American family is being attacked, debased, maligned, slandered, and vilified by every facet of society. *Who Killed the American Family* reveals the concerted assault on the American nuclear family by many forces—feminists, judges, lawmakers, psychologists, college professors, politicians seeking votes, and more—opposed to the traditional American nuclear family, each with its own raison d'etre for wanting to abolish it.

WND Books • A *WND* COMPANY • WASHINGTON DC • WNDBOOKS.COM

PRESENTS

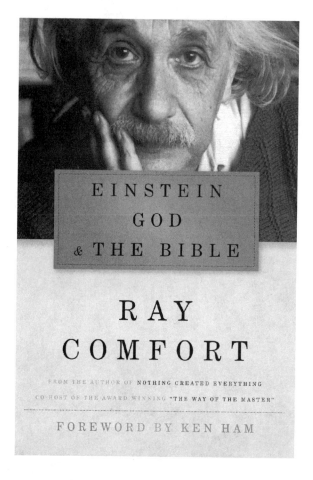

EINSTEIN
GOD
& THE BIBLE

RAY
COMFORT

FROM THE AUTHOR OF **NOTHING CREATED EVERYTHING**
CO-HOST OF THE AWARD WINNING "THE WAY OF THE MASTER"

FOREWORD BY KEN HAM

Was Albert Einstein an atheist? Many celebrity atheist websites claim Einstein as their own, but what did the genius scientist really believe? In *Einstein, God, and the Bible*, international evangelist and best-selling author Ray Comfort explores the mysterious life of this great scientist. Putting to rest once and for all the questions about Einstein's beliefs, Comfort presents a strong case in Einstein's own words for the existence of God.

WND Books · A **WND** COMPANY · WASHINGTON DC · WNDBOOKS.COM

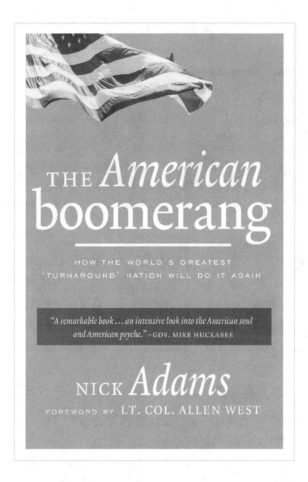

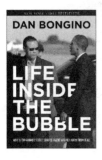
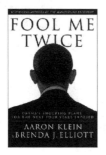

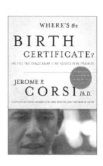

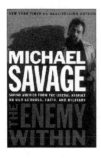
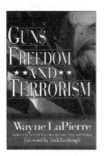
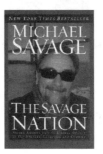